INSTANT BIBLE Dramas

Easy Skits for Elementary Kids

INSTANT BIBLE Dramas

Easy Skits for Elementary Kids

Nick Ransom

Abingdon Press™

Nashville

INSTANT BIBLE DRAMAS
EASY SKITS FOR ELEMENTARY KIDS

ISBN: 9781501821103

PACP10041875-01

Editor: Leigh Meekins
Production Editor: Julie P. Glass
Designer: Jim Carlton

Art—p. 7: Mark Whitaker/MTW Design.net

16 17 18 19 20 21 22 23 24 25—10 9 8 7 6 5 4 3 2 1

Printed in the United States of America

Contents

Contents

Walking on

How to Use Instant Dramas

For the past few years, instant dramas have become a favorite in our children's ministry. Kids in kindergarten–fifth grade equally enjoy the challenge of acting out a story with little to no prep and becoming "experts" in the field of impromptu. The audience also enjoys watching their peers give their take on the story. The dramas in this book have been battle-tested and used within our ministry, but of course as with anything you purchase, you'll need to tweak it to make it work in your setting.

Instant dramas are extremely simple ways to creatively engage your elementary kids in a Bible story. These skits require very little prep, yet engage your kids from kindergarten–fifth grade in the story. If you have extra prep time, you can add great props and kick everything up a notch!

As you invite volunteers to take part in the drama, assign them each a part with the simple instruction that whatever their character is described as doing, they must do. After that, recruit the characters and begin reading the script SLOWLY so the kiddos can act out what they hear. Here are a few tips to use these dramas effectively.

1. Read the script SLOWLY with lots of emotion, allowing time for the participants to hear and interpret the story in their own way. If the kiddos are a little slow to catch on, repeating lines is OK. Take pauses in reading to allow the action to happen.

2. Take five minutes before your teaching time to read over the script and grab any props that will make the story more meaningful. Most props are flexible and optional, so have fun with it.

3. Most times the drama will be interpreted totally different than what you expect. As long as the kids are staying in the spirit of the story, allow them to interpret it the way they want. This is half the fun of the drama.

4. These dramas take a little creative liberty with the story, so be sure to have some follow-up discussion about the exact details of

the story before moving to the next portion of your time. We use instant dramas as a way to introduce the Bible story to the kids.

5. It is suggested that after the drama is complete, read the Scripture for the day so the children hear the Word of God read.

6. At the end of each drama will be two wonder questions. You can use these questions to begin the follow-up discussion. The follow-up discussion can happen as a large group or in smaller groups.

Finally, as you utilize these dramas in your children's ministries, have fun! There is no rehearsal needed for these dramas, and the narrator tells the actors what to do for the action. This is a great opportunity to involve children who may not always get involved in what is happening. Also, this is a fabulous opportunity to involve children of all ages.

Solomon's Job

CHARACTERS: Solomon, David, Construction Workers
SCRIPTURE: 1 Kings 6
PROPS: crown, papers, hard hats/construction gear

Now entering the room is King Solomon. Watch as Solomon takes a bow! Solomon is a very smart king who follows God. Watch as Solomon points to the sky. Solomon has been given a huge job by God and his father, David.

Watch as father David enters the room carrying a very big pile of papers. David hands the papers to Solomon, pats him on the back, points to the sky, and then waves goodbye.

Solomon has been given the job of building the Temple for God. The Temple was kinda like a big church. Solomon looks at the papers and then makes a big confused face. Now watch as Solomon looks at the papers again and then claps his hands.

Now entering the room are the construction workers; watch as they give King Solomon some fist bumps. This is a huge job, so Solomon is going to need a lot of help. Watch as Solomon leaves the room. Watch as the workers look at the papers and then get to work. They saw some wood, hammer some nails, do the robot dance, and paint the wall.

Halftime! Watch as Solomon enters the room and begins inspecting the work so far. Watch as he scratches his head, rubs his beard, and gives the workers a thumbs-up. Now get back to work!

Watch as the workers look at the papers and then get to work. They saw some wood, hammer some nails, do the robot dance, and paint the walls.

A few weeks later, Solomon walks back in to inspect the workers' job. Watch as Solomon looks very closely at the building, then says, "Get back to work." Now watch as Solomon leaves the room.

Watch as the workers look at the papers and then get to work. They saw some wood, hammer some nails, do the robot dance, and paint the walls.

This goes on for a long time. Finally, after seven long years, the Temple is finally finished.

Now entering the room is Solomon. Solomon is so happy; watch as he jumps high in the sky! I mean, really high in the sky. Then Solomon pats all the construction workers on their heads.

The Temple was going to be an awesome place where people could come and worship God. It was a good thing Solomon acted on God's instructions and got to work!

Great job, everyone. Let's cheer for our actors!

Discussion Questions

1. How do you think Solomon felt being in charge of building the Temple?

2. How do you think the people felt when the Temple was completed?

Samuel

CHARACTERS: Samuel, Jesse, 7 Sons of Jesse, David
SCRIPTURE: 1 Samuel 16:1-13
PROPS: empty cup or closed bottle of oil

Now entering the room is the prophet Samuel. Let's cheer for Samuel! God had spoken to Samuel and told him that the Israelite people needed a new king. Watch as Samuel nods his head yes and gives a big thumbs-up. God told Samuel to go to Bethlehem; watch as Samuel begins walking in place.

When Samuel gets to Bethlehem, he does just as God had told him and goes to see a guy named Jesse. Watch as Jesse enters the room and shakes Samuel's hand. Jesse has eight sons; watch as Jesse holds up eight fingers. Watch as Samuel moves his mouth up and down, and waves his arms around; he is asking Jesse if he can meet his sons. Watch as Jesse nods his head yes.

So one by one, Jesse's sons enter the room; watch as they begin entering. Each time one enters the room, he shows off his big muscles and beautiful smile. Watch as the sons smile big and flex their muscles.

Watch as the sons walk toward Samuel. Samuel walks around the sons, inspecting them. Then Samuel gives the crowd a big thumbs-up. These are some good-looking kids.

But wait! God is speaking to Samuel; watch as Samuel pulls on his ear. God is telling Samuel: "These sons are not the ones I'm looking for; ask Jesse if he has another son."

So Samuel moves his mouth up and down, and waves his arms around. He is asking Jesse if he has any more sons. Watch as Jesse nods his head yes and points out the window.

You see, Jesse's last son, David, was out in the field watching over the sheep. It would take at least an hour for him to get here, and you probably wouldn't want David as the king; he is the youngest kid and can barely drive a tractor.

But Samuel waited for David to get there; watch as Samuel sits down, scratches his head, stands up, touches his toes, looks at the clock, walks to the left and then to the right, then he stops and looks at the door. Watch now as David enters the room; he is the one waving to the crowd right now.

Yes, this is the one God has chosen. David will be the next king of Israel; watch as Samuel pours some oil over David's head. The oil is a sign that in a few short years, David will be set apart to be king of Israel.

Watch as Samuel gives David a big thumbs-up.

It didn't matter to God that David wasn't the oldest or didn't have the biggest muscles; what mattered most to God was David's heart and that David tried to do the right thing and follow God.

Great job, everyone. Let's cheer for our actors!

Discussion Questions

1. How do you think Samuel felt anointing the next king?
2. How do you think David felt being anointed as the next king?

Psalm 23

CHARACTERS: Shepherd, Sheep
SCRIPTURE: Psalm 23
PROPS: binoculars, paper bag with a bag of pretzels and bottles of water in it, blanket

Now entering the room is a shepherd. Watch as the shepherd waves to the crowd, smiles big, and then claps his or her hands.

A shepherd watches over sheep, so watch as a bunch of sheep enter the room. Those sheep are so cute! Watch as the sheep give their shepherd some fist bumps and then baa really loudly.

Being a shepherd is a pretty important job in Bible times. Let's see what a shepherd does to take care of her or his sheep.

First, a shepherd has to look for food and water for his or her sheep. Watch as the shepherd walks to the other side of the room and looks over the meadow with her or his binoculars. Watch as the shepherd runs to the corner of the room and picks up a paper bag. What did the shepherd find? Now watch as the shepherd claps his or her hands and calls the sheep.

Watch as the sheep come skipping over. Watch as the shepherd reaches into the bag and hands the sheep some water and pretzels for dinner. YUM!

Second, the shepherd has to protect the sheep from crazy animals. Watch as the shepherd walks over to the other side of the room and begins looking over the meadow with the binoculars. Now watch as the shepherd shows off her or his best ninja moves and air-fights a mean bear!

Now watch as the sheep come skipping over and give their shepherd high-fives.

Third, the shepherd has to find a nice cozy place for the sheep to sleep every night. Watch as the shepherd walks to the other side of the room and looks over the meadow with his or her binoculars. Now watch as the shepherd claps her or his hands and calls the sheep. Watch as the sheep say baa and walk over. Watch as the shepherd grabs a blanket and tosses it at the sheep. Watch as the sheep yawn big! I mean, really big! I mean, really, really big. Then the sheep lie down and go to sleep.

Finally, the shepherd is always with the sheep. The shepherd never leaves the sheep, no matter what football game is on TV, no matter how cold it is outside. The shepherd never leaves.

Why am I telling you all this? Because King David compared God to our Shepherd. A Shepherd who will never leave us. A Shepherd who loves us a whole bunch. God is our Shepherd, and we are the sheep.

Great job, everyone. Let's cheer for our actors!

Discussion Questions
1. How do you think the shepherd feels taking care of the sheep?
2. How does this skit make you feel about the shepherd?

Nehemiah Rebuilds

INSTANT DRAMA

CHARACTERS: Nehemiah, Workers, Mean Person, King
SCRIPTURE: Book of Nehemiah
PROPS: cup of water, crown

Now walking into the room is Nehemiah. Watch as Nehemiah smiles big and waves to the crowd. Nicely done, Nehemiah! Nehemiah was a cupbearer, which meant he sampled the king's drinks to be sure they were safe. Watch as he takes a drink and then gives everyone a big thumbs-up.

One day Nehemiah hears some really bad news. Watch as he gives the crowd two big thumbs-down. He hears the walls to his hometown city, Jerusalem, have been destroyed. This made Nehemiah really sad. Watch as he makes a big sad face. What should Nehemiah do?

Well, the Bible tells us that Nehemiah spends time praying. Watch as Nehemiah gets on his knees and begins praying. The Bible says he does this a long time. Let's wait as time passes, ticktock, ticktock.

OK, that is enough time. Now entering the room is the king. Watch as the king jumps real high! Now watch as Nehemiah moves his mouth up and down, and waves his arms around. He is asking the king if he can take some vacation to go back and rebuild the walls.

Watch as the king scratches his beard, then his head, and then his beard. Listen as the king says, "Yes!" This makes Nehemiah very happy! Watch as he jumps up and down. The king waves goodbye and leaves the room.

Now watch as Nehemiah walks to Jerusalem. He is ready to get this job started. Watch as Nehemiah walks in place.

When Nehemiah arrives, he claps his hands and out comes a bunch of workers. Watch as the workers give each other some fist bumps and then give Nehemiah high-fives.

The workers start building. Watch as they saw some wood. Watch as they hammer some nails. Watch as they do the robot dance. Then watch as they paint the walls.

There were some people who think Nehemiah is crazy for trying to do this. Watch as a mean person enters the room. See the mean person point at Nehemiah and begin laughing. There is no way this wall will ever be finished. Watch as Nehemiah points to the door, and out goes the mean person.

The workers are building. Watch as they saw some wood. Watch as they hammer some nails. Watch as they do the robot dance. Then watch as they paint the walls.

Finally, after 52 days, the walls are finished. Everyone is so excited, they give each other high-fives. Nehemiah knows God is with them. Watch as he gives the crowd a thumbs-up and points to the sky.

Great job, everyone. Let's cheer for our actors!

Discussion Questions

1. How do you think Nehemiah felt when he saw the Temple walls down?

2. How do you think Nehemiah felt watching the walls be built?

Moses & Burning Bush

CHARACTERS: Moses, Sheep, Bush
SCRIPTURE: Exodus 3
PROPS: water bottle, box of cereal, bush cutout with flames

Now entering the room is Moses the shepherd and some of his awesome sheep. Watch as Moses waves! Listen as the sheep baa really loudly! Listen as Moses counts his sheep.

Being a shepherd is actually pretty boring. Every day it is the same old routine. First, Moses gives the sheep some water; watch as he hands them a water bottle. Then Moses makes the sheep dinner; watch as he hands them a box of cereal. Then Moses listens as the sheep baa really loudly! That is pretty much all sheep do.

After feeding the sheep, Moses walks around the stage with them, making sure they are staying together and safe. Then after a long day, Moses and the sheep lie down and go to sleep. Being a shepherd is actually really, really, really boring.

But one day, something crazy happens! Watch as Moses and the sheep stand up.

Now entering the room is a cute little bush, but it is on fire! Yikes! Watch as the sheep run out of the room; they don't like fire.

But wait! Something weird is happening with this bush—even though it is on fire, it is not burning up. Watch as Moses touches the bush, but does not get hurt. This is weird.

Then all of a sudden, a voice speaks: "Moses, this is God. I want you to move!"

Moses is surprised; watch as he makes a big surprised face! Now watch as the bush makes an awesome ninja move.

"Moses, I want you to go to Egypt and free my people from slavery. They are not being treated kindly. I want you to free them and take them to a new land that I promised to give them."

Moses is not so sure about this job. Watch as he shrugs his shoulders and points at himself. But God says, "I will be with you; it will be OK."

Now Moses is confused. Which way is Egypt? Watch as the bush points the way.

Watch as Moses says goodbye to all his sheep and heads off to Egypt.

Great job, everyone. Let's cheer for our actors!

Discussion Questions

1. How do you think you would feel if you saw a burning bush?
2. How would you feel if God asked you to save the people?

Joseph

INSTANT DRAMA

CHARACTERS: Joseph, 11 Brothers, Slave Trader, Potiphar, Police
SCRIPTURE: Genesis 37–41
PROPS: fake or real money, broom

Ever had a bad day or a bad week? What about twenty bad years? Now entering the room is Joseph. Let's all cheer for Joseph! Joseph is waving hello. The story of Joseph is found in the Bible in the Book of Genesis. Joseph had eleven brothers. Watch as the brothers enter the room right now.

Joseph's brothers are not very nice; in fact, they are pretty mean to him. Watch as the brothers make big mean faces. The brothers decide to sell Joseph into slavery. Watch as a young slave trader enters the room and begins to inspect Joseph. The trader checks Joseph's hair, ears, and nose. Now watch as the trader gives the brothers a thumbs-up.

Now watch as the trader hands the brothers some cash. The trader will take Joseph with him to Egypt and get some cash for him.

Watch as the brothers wave goodbye to Joseph, pat Joseph on the back, and head out of the room. Finally, they have gotten rid of their annoying little brother.

Once Joseph arrives in Egypt, he becomes a slave in Potiphar's home. Watch as Potiphar enters the room and gives the trader some cash. Now watch as the trader leaves the room counting his or her money.

Potiphar puts Joseph to work washing the floors and scrubbing the walls. Watch as Joseph sweeps the floor. Joseph does a great job, and Potiphar is happy. Watch as Potiphar gives everyone a big thumbs-up.

All is going great until one day, Joseph is arrested. Watch as the police enter the room.

Joseph is confused; watch as Joseph makes a big confused face.

Joseph is being arrested for doing the right thing! Watch as Potiphar leaves the room and makes a big mad face. He is not happy with Joseph.

Poor Joseph. For thirteen years, Joseph sits in jail. Watch as he makes a big sad face. Even though times are tough for Joseph and Joseph is scared, he still remembers that God is with him. Watch as Joseph points to the sky.

Finally, a day comes when Joseph will be freed from prison and will help save thousands of people. Watch as Joseph skips out of the room.

Great job, everyone. Let's cheer for our actors!

Discussion Questions

1. How do you think Joseph felt being so disliked by his brothers?

2. How do you think Joseph felt living in a very different place?

Jonah Runs Away

INSTANT DRAMA

CHARACTERS: Jonah, Sailors, Ninevites
SCRIPTURE: Jonah 1:1-16
PROPS: none

Now entering the room is Jonah. Let's all cheer for Jonah! Jonah is a prophet, which means God speaks to Jonah and Jonah gives the people God's message. Watch as Jonah points to the sky and then points to his heart.

One day God gave a message to Jonah. Watch as Jonah pulls on his ears. But Jonah did not like this message. Watch as he shakes his head no!

Now entering the room are the Ninevites. Watch as they make big mean faces and give everyone a big thumbs-down! The Ninevites are very mean. They never smile and always laugh at people. Watch as they point to the crowd and laugh.

God wants Jonah to go tell these people about God's love. But Jonah says no. God asks Jonah nicely, "Pretty please," but Jonah says no! In fact, Jonah waves goodbye to the Ninevites and goes in the opposite direction. Watch as the Ninevites leave the room, and Jonah walks in place.

Jonah gets on a boat with some sailors; watch as Jonah points to the door and in walks some sailors. Watch as Jonah moves his mouth up and down, and waves his arms around. He is asking the sailors if he can get a ride on their boat.

Watch as the sailors move their mouths up and down, and wave their arms around. Now watch as the sailors nod their heads yes! Watch as Jonah and the sailors get into the boat and begin rowing. Watch as they row up and down and all around. Watch as they row faster, then slower, then slower, then faster.

Jonah is not following God's direction; in fact, he is doing the opposite. God needs to get his attention, so God sends a big storm. Listen as the crowd makes the sound of thunder. The thunder gets really loud! I mean, really loud.

Then there was lightning; watch as the lights are flashed off and on. Everyone on the boat is really scared. Watch as the sailors make big scared faces. Jonah is actually not scared; in fact, he is asleep. Watch as Jonah lies down and begins snoring very loudly!

Now watch as the sailors run to Jonah and wake him up! Watch as they move their mouths up and down, and wave their arms around. They are telling Jonah about the huge storm. Watch as Jonah stands up and points to the sky. He knows that God is trying to get his attention. Listen as Jonah yells, "Throw me into the water." Watch as the sailors make big confused faces.

What will happen next?! We will have to wait to find out.

Great job, everyone. Let's cheer for our actors!

Discussion Questions
1. How do you think Jonah felt running away from God?
2. How do you think Jonah felt telling the sailors to throw him overboard?

Jonah in the Fish

CHARACTERS: Jonah, Ninevites, Big Fish
SCRIPTURE: Jonah 2–3
PROPS: cutout of fish to make fish character look fishy

Now entering the room is Jonah. Let's all cheer for Jonah! If you remember last time, Jonah got a message from God. Watch as Jonah points to the sky. But Jonah disobeyed God. Watch as Jonah shakes his head no. Jonah went the opposite direction and got on a boat.

Now entering the room is a big fish. Let's cheer for the fish! Watch as the fish swims to the left and then to the right. This fish seems pretty cool! Watch as the fish gives everyone a big thumbs-up. But there was something special about this fish. God has created it to swallow up Jonah. Watch as the fish stands in front of Jonah!

Watch as Jonah looks around the fish and makes a big sad face. Being in a fish's stomach is no fun at all. Watch as Jonah shakes his head no. Being in the fish is stinky and dark. Watch as Jonah plugs his nose, and some of the lights go off in the room. Jonah will be in the fish for three long days. Watch as Jonah holds up three fingers.

Watch as the fish swims to the left and then to the right. Finally, Jonah has a good idea. Watch as he gives the crowd a big thumbs-up. He has decided he is going to pray to God. Watch as Jonah gets on his knees and moves his mouth up and down.

Jonah is telling God he is sorry for not obeying God; he is sorry for running away and will go to Nineveh to tell the people about God.

This was a good prayer! Watch as the fish gives Jonah a high-five and a thumbs-up. Now watch as the fish swims to the left and then to the right. This is making Jonah scared. Watch as he makes a big scared face.

Then all of a sudden, the fish spits Jonah onto dry land. Actually, watch as the fish gently pushes Jonah to one side of the room. There is no spitting in our space today! Watch as the fish leaves and waves goodbye.

Jonah wastes no time. Watch as Jonah walks to the left and then to the right and then to the left. Finally, Jonah has made it to Nineveh.

Now entering the room are the Ninevites. Remember, they are pretty mean people. Watch as they make big mean faces and give everyone a big thumbs-down. Now watch as Jonah moves his mouth up and down, and waves his arms around. He is telling the Ninevites that there is a God who loves them and wants them to do the right thing.

Now watch as the Ninevites scratch their heads and then say, "Tell me more." Now watch as Jonah moves his mouth up and down, and waves his arms around. He is telling the Ninevites that God always hears their prayers, forgives them when they mess up, and really wants them to go around helping others in need. This sounds good to the Ninevites; watch as they give Jonah a big thumbs-up!

Now watch as the Ninevites get on their knees and pray to God. They are going to follow God!

Great job, everyone. Let's cheer for our actors!

Discussion Questions
1. How would you have felt being in the belly of a fish?
2. How would you have felt when the Ninevites prayed to God?

Jesus Is Coming

CHARACTERS: Isaiah, Friend 1, Friend 2, Mary, Joseph
SCRIPTURE: Isaiah 9:6
PROPS: none

"A child is born to us, a son is given to us." Whoa, let's back up a little bit. Did you know that prophets of God predicted that the Messiah, Jesus, would be born? So let's rewind this story a little bit.

Let's watch as the prophet Isaiah walks into the room. Wave to us, Isaiah. Isaiah is a prophet of God, which means he receives messages from God and tells those messages to the people.

Watch as Isaiah gets down on his knees and begins to pray. Go ahead, Isaiah. See Isaiah pull on his ear; he is listening to God. I wonder what God is telling him.

Now watch as Friend 1 enters the room. He is just walking around and looking at the ceiling. Now watch as Isaiah taps Friend 1 on the shoulder and says, "Jesus is coming!"

What great news! See Friend 1 smile. He is so happy, he can't wait.

Now watch as Friend 2 enters the room, waves to the crowd, and then begins skipping. Now watch as Isaiah taps Friend 2 on the shoulder and says, "Jesus is coming!"

What great news! See Friend 2 smile, and jump up and down. She is so happy, she can't wait.

Now Jesus wasn't going to born anytime soon; in fact, it was going to be a very long time before Jesus was born. Watch as Isaiah, Friend 1, and Friend 2 check their watches, check them again, and then check them again.

God's promise to Isaiah was kept, and many years later Mary and Joseph traveled to Bethlehem where Jesus was born. Watch as Mary and Joseph enter the room and wave and smile. They are happy because Jesus has been born. God's promise was kept.

All of us have to wait a few more weeks until it is Christmas. During this time, let's remember that God's promises are always kept and Jesus was born to save us.

Great job, everyone. Let's give our actors a hand!

Discussion Questions

1. How do you think Isaiah felt hearing from God?
2. How do you feel that God's promise was kept?

Jeremiah

CHARACTERS: Jeremiah; Warnings 1, 2, 3, 4
SCRIPTURE: Jeremiah 19
PROPS: "Live Right" sign, handcuffs picture, clay pot, clay pot pieces

Now entering the room is the prophet Jeremiah; watch as Jeremiah waves to the crowd! Jeremiah is a prophet, which means he gets messages from God and then shares those messages with others. Watch as Jeremiah points to the sky and then points to his ear.

The message that Jeremiah has for the people is a warning. Watch as Jeremiah holds out his hand like a stop sign. Now watch as Jeremiah points to the door.

Entering the room is Warning 1. This sign being carried in says to live right. Jeremiah wants the people to be kind to each other and take care of each other—don't just come to church, but live the right way.

Now watch as Jeremiah holds up two fingers and then points to the door. Here comes Warning 2. Warning 2 is a picture of handcuffs. Jeremiah told the people that if they didn't live right, they would one day be slaves or handcuffed to their enemies.

Now watch as Jeremiah holds up three fingers and then points to the door. Here comes Warning 3. Warning 3 is a clay pot in one piece and a clay pot in many pieces. Jeremiah tells the people that unless they live right, their town will be in many pieces, like this broken pottery.

Still, the people of Israel are not listening. Watch as Jeremiah shakes his head no and makes a big sad face.

The final warning is coming in the door right now.

Watch as this warning walks up to Jeremiah and points at him, then pats Jeremiah on the back. This warning is telling Jeremiah to not stop giving God's message to the people. This warning is saying that God loves the people and wants them to love others too.

Watch as Jeremiah looks to the sky, then gives everyone a big thumbs-up! Jeremiah is going to keep telling everyone the messages that God gives him.

Great job, everyone. Let's cheer for our actors!

Discussion Questions

1. How do you think the people felt hearing Jeremiah's warnings?

2. How do you think the people felt, hearing they must change?

God Provides Manna

INSTANT DRAMA

CHARACTERS: Israelites
SCRIPTURE: Exodus 16
PROPS: snack

Now marching around the room are the Israelites. Let's cheer for the Israelites! The Israelites had been wandering around the wilderness for a long time; watch as they check their watches, look around the room, and then keep marching.

The Israelites had been slaves in Egypt. They had worked hard and got paid nothing. God does not like slavery. So God freed the Israelites and was taking them to a new home. But God had to teach them a few things first.

Now watch as the Israelites march to the front of the room. The Israelites are tired. See them rub their heads and yawn really big. They are also hungry. See them rub their bellies. They are so hungry that they are mad. Notice the Israelites look mad.

The Israelites have forgotten about God and how God has taken care of them so far. They are angry with God. Watch as they point to the sky and then wave their arms around while making angry faces. Now watch as they rub their bellies; they are so hungry.

Finally, God told the Israelites to go to sleep and in the morning, there would be food for them. Now watch as the Israelites lie on the floor and go to sleep. (Turn off a few lights, if you want.)

(Sing quietly.) Hush, little Israelites, don't say word. In the morning, you will have some food. (Add a simple snack in a container on the floor.)

Soon it is morning, and the Israelites wake up. They are still hungry! Watch as they rub their bellies.

Wait! What is that on the ground next to them? Watch as they pick up the food and try it. Now watch as they smile big and say, "Yummy!" It tastes kind of like honey and wafers and bread. The Israelites keep picking up the food, and their bellies start feeling full! The Israelites call the food *manna*.

See? God takes care of the Israelites and provides them with food.

Great job, everyone. Let's cheer for our actors!

Discussion Questions

1. How do you think the people felt when there was manna for food?

2. How do you feel about God providing for the people?

Fiery Furnace

CHARACTERS: King Neb, Shadrach, Meshach, Abednego, Mean Servant, Statue

SCRIPTURE: Daniel 3

PROPS: cool song ready to play that the children will recognize

Now standing on the stage is a statue. Watch as the statue waves hello. Now watch as the statue jumps up and down. Wait. It can't do any of these things; it's just a statue. But this statue was very important to one person, and his name was King Nebuchadnezzar. Watch as the king enters the room and everyone in the crowd cheers for the king.

One day King Neb has an idea. Watch as he scratches his head and points to the sky. Neb decides to build a really awesome statue; watch as he points to the statue. Then Neb has another awesome idea; watch as Neb holds up two fingers. Neb decides that whenever his favorite song plays, everyone would stop what he or she is doing and bow down. Can anyone guess what King Neb's favorite song is? Watch as King Neb demonstrates; when the music plays, watch as the king bows down.

Very nice, king. Everyone in the whole kingdom is supposed to bow down when they hear this beautiful song. But there are three people who would not bow down to anyone but the one true God.

Now entering the room are Shadrach, Meshach, and Abednego. Watch as they wave to the crowd. Shadrach, Meshach, and Abednego are followers of the one true God. See them point to the sky. God is number one in their lives; watch as they each hold up one finger. Shadrach, Meshach, and Abednego were not going to bow down to the statue. Watch as they shake their heads no.

This makes the king mad. See King Neb make an angry face. But he is going to give Shadrach, Meshach, and Abednego one more chance to bow down. Watch as the king claps his hands, and the music plays one more time. The king bows down, but Shadrach, Meshach, and Abednego do not. Uh-oh. These guys are in big trouble.

Watch as the king points to the door. In walks a very mean servant. Check out this guy's angry face. King Neb begins moving his mouth up and down, and waving his arms around. He is telling his servant to throw these three dudes into the fiery hot furnace. This is their punishment for not following orders!

Watch as the servant leaves the room with Shadrach, Meshach, and Abednego. Shadrach, Meshach, and Abednego spend the night in a fiery furnace, but you see, they were not alone. Watch as everyone in the crowd holds up four fingers. During the night, a fourth person— an angel of God—shows up and protects Shadrach, Meshach, and Abednego from the fire.

Now watch as Shadrach, Meshach, and Abednego walk back in the room without a single burn mark. See how they are smiling and waving. The king is really surprised at this; watch as the king makes a big surprised face! God protected Shadrach, Meshach, and Abednego, and because of God's protection, King Neb started following the one true God too.

Great job, everyone. Let's cheer for our actors!

Discussion Questions

1. How do you feel about Shadrach, Meshach, and Abednego being thrown in the fiery furnace?
2. How do you think the three friends felt in the furnace?

Esther

CHARACTERS: Queen Esther, Mordecai, King, People/Helpers
SCRIPTURE: Esther 4–7
PROPS: random stuff, crown

Standing in front of you now is Queen Esther. Esther follows God. Watch as she points to the sky. Esther became queen by winning a contest. The contest involved karate kicks, ninja moves, and doing the best robot dance. Actually, it was more of a beauty pageant.

As the queen, Esther also has a lot of helpers. Watch as the helpers enter the room and give her all the stuff she'll need to be queen today. Now watch as the helpers quickly sneak out of the room.

One day Esther hears about a terrible law—a law that is going to hurt a lot of people, the Jewish people. She has to do something; she is the queen. But she is scared. Watch as she makes a big scared face.

Esther grew up with her Uncle Mordecai. Watch as Mordecai enters the room. Mordecai also follows God. Watch as he points to the sky. Mordecai knows Esther is scared. See him give Esther a high-five and get down on his knees. He is praying that Esther will have the courage to talk to the king about the law. After Mordecai is done praying, he gives Esther a thumbs-up and jumps like a kangaroo out of the room.

Now entering the room is the king. Let's all cheer for the king. Watch as the king flexes his muscles. See Esther bow to the king. Now watch as she moves her mouth up and down, and waves her arms. She is telling the king she has something very important to share. Watch as the king pulls on both his ears and listens closely.

But Esther is scared. Watch as she moves her mouth up and down, and waves her arms around. She is telling the king that she would like to share this important thing with him tomorrow. Listen as the king says OK and then leaves the room skipping.

See Mordecai enter the room again. Mordecai still follows God. Watch as he points to the sky. Mordecai knows Esther is scared. Watch as he gives Esther a high-five and gets down on his knees. He is praying that Esther will have the courage to talk to the king about the law tomorrow. After Mordecai is done praying, he gives Esther a thumbs-up and then dances his way out of the room.

It is now tomorrow. Watch as the king enters the room and flexes his muscles. Watch as Esther takes a deep breath, then moves her mouth up and down, and waves her arms around. She is doing it! She is telling the king about the law.

Watch as the king makes a big surprised face! He had no idea about this law and that it would hurt so many people. Listen as the king yells, "I'll fix it," and then runs out of the room.

Now watch as a bunch of people run into the room! They are so happy and thankful for Esther's courage. Watch as they jump up and down, and give each other high-fives. Esther has saved the day.

Great job, everyone. Let's cheer for our actors!

Discussion Questions
1. How do you feel hearing the story of Esther?
2. How do you think Esther felt talking to the king?

Elijah and Elisha

CHARACTERS: Elijah, Elisha, Chariot and 2 Horses
SCRIPTURE: 2 Kings 2:1-14
PROPS: anything to help the cast look like a chariot and horses

Now entering the room is the prophet Elijah; watch as Elijah waves to the crowd and gives everyone a big thumbs-up. Elijah had a follower—his name was Elisha. Watch as Elisha enters the room and stands next to Elijah.

Elisha wants to know everything about Elijah and what it means to follow God. So Elisha follows Elijah everywhere. Watch as Elijah walks to the left side of the room and Elisha follows. See Elijah walk to the right side of the room and Elisha follows. Now watch as Elijah comes back to the center of the room and does three jumping jacks, and Elisha follows.

See Elisha wave his arms around, and move his mouth up and down. Elisha is asking Elijah a question. Watch as Elisha holds up two fingers and then flexes his muscles. Elisha wants a double portion of Elijah's strength and energy to follow God.

Watch as Elijah nods his head yes. Elisha will get a double portion, but only if he sees the cool ride Elijah is about to take. So Elisha keeps following Elijah.

Watch as Elijah walks to the left side of the room and Elisha follows. See Elijah walk to the right side of the room and Elisha follows. Now watch as Elijah comes back to the center of the room and does three jumping jacks, and Elisha follows.

See a flaming chariot race onto the stage and point at Elijah. Watch as Elijah looks around the chariot and gives the chariot a big thumbs-up.

Elijah waves goodbye to Elisha and races off the stage with the chariot.

Elisha is sad that Elijah is gone; watch as Elisha makes a big sad face. But Elisha knows God is with him and that he has lots of work to do for God. Watch as Elisha exits the room.

Great job, everyone. Let's cheer for our actors!

Discussion Questions

1. How do you think Elisha felt following Elijah?
2. How do you feel hearing this story?

David & Mephibosheth

INSTANT DRAMA

CHARACTERS: King David, Servant, Mephibosheth, Gift 1, Gift 2
SCRIPTURE: 2 Samuel 9
PROPS: crown for David, picture of a tree, snacks

Now entering the room is King David; watch as he salutes the crowd. Watch as David sits down and begins to scratch his head. David is doing some thinking. See David clap his hands, and a servant enters the room.

Watch as the servant bows to David. Now watch as David moves his mouth up and down, and waves his arms around. He is asking his servant if there is anyone he could show kindness to today.

Watch as the servant stands up and scratches her or his head. Now watch as the servant runs out of the room and comes back in with a friend named Mephibosheth.

See Mephibosheth slowly walk into the room. You may notice that he is limping. You see, Mephibosheth was dropped as a baby and since that day, he cannot walk very well.

Mephibosheth is very scared to be visiting David. Watch as he makes a big scared face. Mephibosheth is worried that the king is going to throw him into jail because he is related to the old king, King Saul.

But watch as David shakes his head no. David wants to be nice to Mephibosheth. See David give Mephibosheth a big thumbs-up and then some fist bumps.

David has some gifts for Mephibosheth; watch as David points to the door. Now entering the room is Gift 1. It's a big tree! You see, David is giving Mephibosheth a lot of land so he can farm and make a living. See Mephibosheth smile big and give David a high-five.

Watch as David points to the door Now entering the room is Gift 2: a beautiful bag of snacks and food. David has invited Mephibosheth to eat dinner with him anytime he wants to.

See Mephibosheth smile big and give David a high-five.

Now watch as David gives Mephibosheth a handshake and one final gift. Watch as David moves his mouth up and down, and tells Mephibosheth that he will always be his friend. Anytime Mephibosheth needs anything to come ask. This makes Mephibosheth very happy; watch as he gives David a big high-five and yells out a thank-you!

Wow! David showed some extreme kindness in this story. Let's be like David this week and look to show kindness to those around us.

Great job, everyone. Let's cheer for our actors!

Discussion Questions

1. How do you feel about David being so nice to Mephibosheth?

2. How do you think Mephibosheth felt?

Daniel Likes Veggies

CHARACTERS: Daniel, Daniel's 3 Friends, King, Servant
SCRIPTURE: Daniel 1
PROPS: crown, yummy food, fruit & vegetables, water bottle

Now entering the room is Daniel. Let's cheer for Daniel! Daniel also has a few friends. Watch as Daniel points to the door, and his friends come skipping in! Daniel and his friends are a little nervous; watch as they make big scared faces. They are nervous because they are starting a new job.

Let's meet the new boss. The boss is actually the king over all the land as far as anyone can see. Let's cheer as the king enters the room. Watch as the king gives the crowd a thumbs-up and then shakes the hands of Daniel and his friends.

Now watch as the king walks around Daniel and his friends. Watch as the king taps them on their heads and their shoulders.

The king is going to train and test Daniel and his friends for the next few weeks to be his servants. Watch as the king claps his hands, and Daniel and his friends do four jumping jacks. Nicely done! Next, the king claps his hands, and Daniel and his friends must do five toe-touches—1, 2, 3, 4, 5. Great job! Now watch as Daniel and his friends give the king a thumbs-up; they are ready for this training.

See the king move his mouth up and down, and wave his arms around. He is telling Daniel and his friends that they will be doing this strict training for three years! Watch as the king holds up three fingers. This training will involve the mind; watch as the king points to his head. It will also involve their muscles; watch as the king flexes his muscles. It will also involve their bellies!

Yes, that is right—Daniel and his friends will eat the king's food only.

Watch as the king claps his hands and in walks a servant carrying some yummy food. See the king rub his belly and then say, "Yum!"

But wait! Daniel and his friends yell, "No!" Watch as Daniel and his friends move their mouths up and down, and wave their arms around. They are telling the king they can't eat his food. It has been offered to idols, and God does not want them to eat that food. The king is confused; watch as he scratches his head.

See Daniel point to the sky. God is guiding Daniel and his friends, and they want to obey God! Now watch as Daniel claps his hands and the servant runs out and brings back a delicious bag of fruits and veggies!

For the next three years, Daniel and his friends eat fruits and veggies, instead of the king's food. They let God guide them, and they end up super strong and healthy. See Daniel and his friends flex their muscles.

Daniel allowed God to guide him in everything, even in the food he ate.

Great job, everyone. Let's cheer for our actors!

Discussion Questions
1. How do you think Daniel felt eating the healthy food when others were not?
2. How do you think Daniel felt following God?

Daniel & Lions' Den

CHARACTERS: Daniel, 2 Leaders, King
SCRIPTURE: Daniel 6
PROPS: kazoos

Now entering the room is Daniel. Let's cheer for Daniel! Daniel works for the king and also follows God. Watch as Daniel points to the sky.

You know Daniel follows God because he prays three times a day. Every morning Daniel would get on his knees and say a prayer. Now watch as Daniel stands up and walks around. Now it is lunchtime and at lunchtime, Daniel gets on his knees and prays. Now watch as Daniel stands up and walks around. Now it is bedtime and at bedtime, Daniel gets on his knees and prays. Daniel loves to talk to God.

There are a couple of leaders who do not like Daniel. Watch as these leaders enter the room and make big mean faces, then flex their muscles and show off their ninja moves. They want to get Daniel in trouble. But they can't find anything wrong with Daniel. Watch as Daniel stands up, gives some fist bumps to the mean leaders, and then leaves the room. Yikes! Being nice! The leaders couldn't stand it that Daniel was so nice.

Now listen as the leaders blow their kazoos, and the king enters the room. Watch as the king waves and shakes some hands. The king is a pretty cool guy!

See the leaders walk up to the king and move their mouths up and down, and wave their arms around. They are telling the king that he should make a new law that no one is allowed to pray to anyone but the king for the next thirty days. If anyone does not pray to the king, that person will be thrown into the lions' den.

Watch as the king rubs his beard and begins to think. See the king give the leaders a big thumbs-up. He loves the law! Let's do it. Now watch as the king and the leaders leave the stage.

Daniel hears about the law, but that doesn't change anything for him. He is still going to pray to the one true God. Watch as Daniel gets on his knees and begins praying.

See the leaders rush into the room and point at Daniel, and then point at the king. Daniel is breaking the law. The king makes a big sad face. He doesn't want to hurt Daniel, but a law is a law. Watch as the king points off the stage, and the leaders take Daniel to the lions' den.

All night long, the king could not sleep. Watch as the king walks back and forth on the stage. He is worried about Daniel. Once morning arrives, the king runs to the lions' den. Watch as the king runs!

When he gets there, he finds Daniel. See Daniel and the king walk onto the stage. They are both so happy. Watch as they give each other high-fives and fist bumps.

God protected Daniel!

Great job, everyone. Let's cheer for our actors!

Discussion Questions
1. How do you think Daniel felt when the law was passed to only pray to the king?
2. How do you think Daniel felt in the lions' den?

Ruth

CHARACTERS: Naomi, Elimelech, Mahlon, Chilion, Orpah, Ruth, Boaz
SCRIPTURE: Book of Ruth
PROPS: none

Entering the room now is Naomi and her husband, Elimelech. Watch as Naomi and Elimelech do five jumping jacks. Naomi and Elimelech had two children who were also married; watch as Mahlon and Chilion enter the room and give the crowd a big thumbs-up. Mahlon's and Chilion's wives were Orpah and Ruth. See Orpah and Ruth enter the room, smile big, and wave. Life was pretty good for Naomi and her family. See everyone's big smiles! But soon, some really bad stuff began happening.

One day Elimelech got sick. Watch as he begins coughing and coughs some more and coughs a little bit more. Elimelech kept getting sicker and sicker, until one day he died. Watch as Elimelech falls to the ground. This made Noami very sad. See her make a sad face.

But things got worse. A little while later, Mahlon and Chilion got sick and died. Watch as they begin coughing and cough some more, and fall to the floor. This made Ruth and Orpah very sad; watch as they make big sad faces.

Noami decides she is going to move away, back to her hometown of Bethlehem. Watch as Noami moves her mouth up and down, and waves her arms around. She is telling Ruth and Orpah to stay here with their families and find new husbands when they are ready. Watch as Orpah waves goodbye to Ruth. But Naomi leaves with Ruth. See them leave the room. They are going to find a new home in Bethlehem.

Once they get to Bethlehem, Ruth and Naomi are hungry. Watch as they rub their bellies. Ruth decides to head out to a field and pick wheat that was left by the farmers for those in need. Watch as Ruth walks around the room, picking up grains of wheat. While she is doing this, the head farmer of this field named Boaz enters the story. Watch as Boaz walks into the room and waves to the crowd. Then he does two pushups.

Boaz is a very rich, but very caring person. He sees Ruth and over time, gets to know her pretty well. Watch as Ruth and Boaz begin talking. Time passes. See Boaz and Ruth tap their watches. After a few months, Boaz and Ruth end up getting married; see Ruth and Boaz give each other a big high-five. Not only do they get married, but Boaz takes care of Naomi as well.

Watch as Naomi walks up to Boaz and gives him a high-five too. God has some big plans for Ruth and Boaz down the road. In fact, one of their descendants is going to be King David!

Great job, everyone. Let's cheer for our actors!

Discussion Questions

1. How do you think Naomi felt when she and Ruth began to travel back to her home in Bethlehem?

2. How do you think Ruth felt working in the fields and meeting Boaz?

Naaman

INSTANT DRAMA

CHARACTERS: Naaman, Servant Girl, Elisha, Elisha's Servant, Naaman's Servant, Jordan River
SCRIPTURE: 2 Kings 5
PROPS: bag of goodies, blue/brown paper for water

Now standing in front of you is the mighty warrior, Naaman! Watch as he flexes his muscles. Does one jumping jack and then does his best ninja move! Naaman is an excellent soldier, and everyone knows it. Watch as Naaman gives everyone a big thumbs-up. But Naaman has a problem. He is sick with a skin disease. Watch as Naaman begins scratching his arms and then his legs and then his head. He is very itchy! Not only is Naaman itchy, but his skin disease is also very painful. Listen as he yells, "Ouchie! Ouchie!"

This skin disease is serious business, and Naaman is in big trouble. Watch as Naaman makes a big sad face. Naaman has a servant girl. See the servant girl skip over to Naaman. This servant girl follows God. Watch as she points to the sky. The servant girl moves her mouth up and down, and waves her arms around. She is telling Naaman that there is a prophet of God named Elisha. Naaman should visit Elisha. Elisha might be able to help with his disease.

Naaman claps his hands and in walks another servant carrying a bag of goodies. I wonder if Elisha likes donuts. Naaman and his servants walk around the room. As they are walking, Elisha and his messenger enter the room and stand on the stage.

As Naaman and his crew get close, Elisha sends his servant to Naaman. Listen as Elisha yells, "Go now." The servant runs over to Naaman and his crew. Naaman is so excited to see them, he gives the servant a high-five!

Now watch as Naaman moves his mouth up and down, and waves his arms around, and then gives the bag of goodies to Elisha's servant. Elisha's servant sets the bag down and shakes his head no. He doesn't need the bag of goodies. The servant moves his mouth up and down, and waves his arms around. He is telling Naaman that God will heal him if he takes seven baths in the Jordan River!

Now entering the room is the Jordan River! Watch as the river waves to everyone. Wait a minute—why is the river brown and blue? The Jordan River isn't the cleanest river around.

When Naaman hears this, he is mad. Watch as he makes a big mad face. Why does he have to take a bath seven times in a dirty river? Watch as Naaman's servants wave their arms around, and move their mouths up and down. They finally convince Naaman to give it a try.

Watch as Naaman and his crew wave goodbye to Elisha and his servant, and walk to the Jordan River. Naaman walks into the river and goes under the water seven times really fast—1, 2, 3, 4, 5, 6, 7!

On the seventh time, Naaman is healed. See Naaman jump really high in the air! I mean, really high in the air! Now watch as he gives his servants high-fives. God has healed Naaman!

Great job, everyone. Let's cheer for our actors!

Discussion Questions
1. How would you feel if you were told to wash in a dirty river seven times to be healed?
2. How do you think Naaman felt when he was healed?

Water From a Rock

CHARACTERS: Moses, Israelites (3–5 people), Water Delivery Dude
SCRIPTURE: Exodus 17:1-7
PROPS: water bottles, small rock, small stick

Now entering the room are the Israelites. Watch as they wave to the crowd and take a bow. Now watch as the Israelites march to the left and then to the right and then to the left again.

After God freed the Israelites from slavery, God was taking them to their new home in the Promised Land, but the Israelites complained a lot and didn't trust God. So their punishment was to spend more time in the wilderness. Watch as the Israelites make big sad faces.

The wilderness is hot. Watch as the Israelites wipe their heads. It is also tiring to travel around; watch as they yawn big! Soon, the Israelites are thirsty. Watch as they stick out their tongues.

They look around for water, but they don't find anything to drink. This makes them sad. Watch as they make big sad faces. Now listen as the Israelites yell for their leader, Moses!

Now entering the room is Moses; watch as Moses smiles big and does his best ninja move. Watch as the Israelites move their mouths up and down, and wave their arms around. They are complaining to Moses that they are out of water and they are so thirsty.

Moses gets on his knees to pray. God gives a message to Moses. Moses goes and gets a rock, and puts it on the floor. Now watch as Moses leaves and comes back with a stick. God has told Moses to hit the rock, and water will come from the rock.

The Israelites scratch their heads. Is this really what God wants Moses to do? Watch as the Israelites make big confused faces.

Moses grabs the stick and gets into a proper batting stance. Moses bends his knees, and he is ready to hit a home run! Listen as the Israelites count to 3, and then watch Moses hit the rock. Ready—1, 2, 3.

Moses smacks the rock perfectly. Then all of a sudden, in runs a dude with some water bottles. Watch as the dude places the water bottles next to the rock, waves to the Israelites, does a jumping jack, and then leaves the rock. The Israelites are so excited to see water; watch as they jump high in the air! I mean, really high in the air!

The Israelites grab the water bottles and pretend to take a drink. Watch as they give Moses high-fives. Moses points that way. It's time to keep wandering the wilderness. See the Israelites walk to the left and then to the right. This is going to be a long trip.

Great job, everyone. Let's cheer for our actors!

Discussion Questions

1. How do you think the Israelites felt when they were wandering in the wilderness?

2. How do you think God felt when the people were complaining?

Abe's Big Move!

CHARACTERS: Abraham, Sarah, People of Haran, Stars, Cool Dude
SCRIPTURE: Genesis 12:1-9; 15:5-6
PROPS: two suitcases, stars, yummy snacks

Now entering the room is Abraham and Sarah! Watch as they wave to the crowd and give each other a high-five. Abraham and Sarah had a pretty good life; they lived in a place called Haran. Haran was a nice city. See Abraham and Sarah give everyone a big thumbs-up.

In Haran, Abraham and Sarah had many friends. Watch as a group of friends enters the room and gives Abraham and Sarah some fist bumps and then leaves the room. In Haran, there were some sweet places to eat! Watch as Abraham and Sarah clap their hands and in walks a cool dude with some yummy snacks. Watch as they give the cool dude high-fives and then take the snacks.

Haran was a pretty sweet place to live, and Abraham and Sarah had lived there a long time. One day God spoke to Abraham. See Abraham point to the sky and then pull on his ear. God asks Abraham to move to a new land! Watch as Abraham makes a big confused face and asks where.

Abraham knows that God will show him where to go. So Abraham and Sarah pack up their stuff; watch as they grab two suitcases and then give each other a big thumbs-up. They are ready to move.

Abraham and Sarah begin walking around the room. It is a long journey, and they aren't sure where they are going, but God is guiding them. Abraham and Sarah check their watches and then keep on walking. Watch as they check their watches again and keep on walking. How much farther? God finally tells Abraham and Sarah to stop!

Watch as Abraham and Sarah stop walking and return to the front of the room. They had followed God and found their new home! Watch as Abraham and Sarah give each other a high-five! But God wasn't finished with Abraham yet. A little while later in the evening, Sarah is sleeping. Watch as Sarah lies on the floor and falls asleep.

Listen as she starts to snore really loudly. She must be really tired. Now listen as Sarah stops snoring! Abraham and Sarah have no kids, and this makes them sad. Watch as Abraham makes a big sad face.

But on this night, God brings Abraham outside and has him look at the sky. Watch as Abraham looks up. Now watch as some stars enter the room. Wow! That is a lot of stars. Watch as the stars do a little robot dance! God tells Abraham that one day, he will have as many descendants as there are stars in the sky. In other words, he will have a really big family! This makes Abraham happy; watch as he smiles big and gives everyone a high-five.

God was pleased with Abraham's faith and how he had acted. God did eventually bless Abraham with a huge family!

Great job, everyone. Let's cheer for our actors!

Discussion Questions
1. How do you think Abraham and Sarah felt when God told them to move?
2. How do you think Abraham and Sarah felt in the new land?

The Tower of Babel

CHARACTERS: Construction Workers, God
SCRIPTURE: Genesis 11
PROPS: construction hats, plastic construction tools (optional)

Now entering the room are some very cool construction workers! Watch as they take a bow and flex their muscles. Watch as the construction workers rub their chins and then scratch their heads. What to build? What to build? They got it! Watch as everyone points to the ceiling. They will build a large tower! It will be very tall.

The construction workers jump high in the air. No, I mean really high in the air. No, jump really high in the air! This is going to be a tall tower. Now watch as the construction workers fold their arms and act all cool. When people see their tower, they will remember how cool these workers were!

See the construction workers get to work. Watch as they hammer some nails, saw some wood, and paint the walls. This tower is really taking shape. There is nothing wrong with the construction workers building a tower, except for the fact it was filling them with pride and they weren't really following God's law.

But the construction workers keep on working. Watch as they hammer some nails, saw some wood, and paint the walls. This tower is really taking shape.

Finally, it is break time; watch as the construction workers wipe their heads. Now they take a look at their tower again. It is looking pretty awesome! See the construction workers give each other a big thumbs-up.

The Bible says that God came to visit the tower. Watch as God enters the room and shakes hands with all the construction workers. God walks around, looking at the tower. Now watch as God waves goodbye and leaves the room.

Well, time to get back work; watch as the construction workers move their mouths up and down, and wave their arms around. See the construction workers make big confused faces! They can't understand what the other person is saying. They try again. Watch as the construction workers move their mouths up and down, and wave their arms around. They still cannot understand each other, so the construction workers just stand around and look at each other.

See the construction workers make funny faces at each other. Now watch as they just smile at each other. Watch as the construction workers shake hands and wave goodbye. I guess they'll head in different directions now. The tower will have to stay unfinished for now—which is what God wanted all along.

Great job, everyone. Let's cheer for our actors!

Discussion Questions
1. How do you think God felt about the tower and the construction workers?
2. How do you feel about everyone having a different language?

Peter and John

INSTANT DRAMA

CHARACTERS: Lame Person, Peter, John, Friends
SCRIPTURE: Acts 3:1-10
PROPS: none

Good afternoon, ladies and gentlemen. Welcome to the 3 o'clock news! We are here at the Temple in front of the Beautiful Gate.

Sitting in front of the gate is a man who cannot walk; watch as the man tries to stand and then falls over again. The poor man has never been able to walk. This is very sad. See the man make a sad face.

Every day the man sits in front of the gate asking for money from people. Watch as the man holds out his hands asking for money.

It just so happens that two of Jesus' followers, Peter and John, are coming to the Temple to pray. Watch as Peter and John walk in the room. Wave to us, Peter and John! Just as Peter and John are about to enter the Temple, they notice the lame man and walk over to him.

Watch as Peter begins talking to the lame man; watch as Peter moves his mouth up and down. Now watch the lame man move his mouth up and down as he talks to Peter and John. See John move his mouth up and down as he talks to Peter and the lame man. I wonder what they are saying.

The lame man has asked for some money from Peter and John. Watch as Peter and John look for money in their pockets, but they don't have any. Watch as Peter and John shake their heads no.

The lame man is sad and makes a big sad face. But wait! Peter has an idea. See Peter point to the sky. Peter and John tell the lame man they don't have any money, but they have something better.

See Peter and John each hold out one hand toward the lame man. What are they doing? They hold hands with the lame man and ask him to stand up. The lame man is a little confused and makes a big confused face. But he is going to try to stand up. The lame man slowly begins to stand and, look! He is doing it. The man can stand and walk; he is healed. He is so happy!

See the lame man smile and give Peter and John high-fives. He is so excited! Watch the lame man jump up and down, praising God. Look as his friends are running in; they can't believe what has just happened. See their excited faces.

What a party! The lame man is so thankful to God. He is still jumping and praising God. He must be tired by now!

Watch everyone leave the room.

Great job, everybody. Let's give our actors a big hand!

Discussion Questions

1. How do you think the lame man felt not being able to walk?
2. How do you think Peter and John felt sharing the miracle with the lame man?

Fruit of the Spirit

INSTANT DRAMA

CHARACTERS: 9 Fruit of the Spirit
SCRIPTURE: Galatians 5:22-23
PROPS: none

Now entering the room are our terrific actors and actresses. Let's cheer loud as these friends enter the room! We are talking about fruit, but not the kind of fruit you eat; watch as our friends shake their heads no. But the kind of fruit the Bible says our lives should produce when we follow Jesus.

Let's meet the fruit of the Spirit.

The first fruit of the Spirit is Love. Watch as our friend points to his or her heart and then points to you. When we follow Jesus, we should show love to everyone!

The second fruit is Joy. Watch as our friend smiles big and shows all her or his teeth; she or he is super happy! When we follow Jesus, our lives our filled with joy!

Fruit number three is Peace. Watch as our friend holds up two fingers and gives everyone the peace sign. Peace means we try and get along with everyone and not cause trouble.

Up next is Patience. Watch as our friend looks at his or her watch and then taps his or her feet. Being patient means we can wait and not get grumpy about it. See how happy our friend looks!

Moving on to fruit number five which is Kindness. Watch as our friend smiles big and walks around saying kind things to others. Listen as she or he says, "You are pretty cool" and "Nice job on the skit so far." There are many ways to be kind, but making sure only kind words come out of our mouths is a great place to start.

The next fruit is Goodness. Watch as our friend gives everyone a big thumbs-up! Goodness simply means finding out what God thinks is good and doing it.

Fruit number seven is Faithfulness. Watch as our friend huddles up with others. Faithfulness means sticking together and not giving up just because things are hard. We should be faithful to God because God is faithful to us.

Fruit number eight is Gentleness. Watch as our friend carefully picks up a little puppy from the floor and begins ever so carefully petting it. (Just so you know, our puppy is invisible.) Good puppy! It is so cute! Not only should we be gentle with our actions, but also with our words—always thinking of how others feel if we act or speak a certain way.

Finally, we come to Self-control. Watch as our friend holds up his or her hand like a stop sign. Self-control is being able to handle your emotions and actions, even when things don't go your way.

The Bible says that as we follow Jesus, our lives should show more of these fruit.

Great job, everyone. Let's cheer for our actors!

Discussion Questions
1. How do you feel about fruit of the Spirit?
2. How do you think you can practice fruit of the Spirit?

Holy Week

CHARACTERS: As Many As You Want
SCRIPTURE: Mark 11–16
PROPS: none

Now entering the room are some amazing actors and actresses who will help us tell the story of this most amazing week, Holy Week. Let's give this crew five loud claps!

Jesus enters the city of Jerusalem; everyone is so excited to see him. Watch as the group smiles big and gives each other high-fives. The crowd waves palm branches and shouts, "Hosanna!" Listen as the group waves their arms in the air and then shouts, "Hosanna!"

A few days later, Jesus and his disciples eat a meal together. See the group rub their bellies and begin chewing. This is not your regular meal; it is the celebration of the Passover and Jesus' last meal with the disciples. Watch as the group bows their heads and closes their eyes. They are remembering the love of Jesus.

At this meal, Jesus also washes everyone's feet. Watch as the group points to their feet.

That night Jesus is arrested and put on trial. After the trial, Jesus is sent to die on the cross. How very sad. Watch as the group makes big sad faces.

Jesus loves us so much. Watch as the group stretches their arms from side to side to show how big Jesus' love is for us.

The next couple of days are very quiet and sad. See each group member raise one finger and cover his or her mouth to make a "Shhh" sign. The people wait for what would happen next. Watch as the group looks at their watches and then looks at their watches again.

On Sunday, a few people go to see where Jesus is buried. Watch as the group walks in place. When they get to the tomb, they are surprised. Watch as they make big surprised faces.

Jesus is not in the tomb. Jesus is alive. He has risen from the dead! At first, the group is confused; watch as they scratch their heads. Then they see Jesus. See the group point. When they see Jesus, they are so excited! Watch as the group jumps up and down.

The group is so excited that they run out of the room to tell everyone they can. The news that Jesus is alive begins to spread from person to person to person. Today we know the good news. Jesus is alive!

Great job, everyone. Let's cheer for our actors!

Discussion Questions

1. How do you think the people felt seeing Jesus enter Jerusalem?
2. How do you feel hearing this story?

Thomas Sees Jesus

INSTANT DRAMA

CHARACTERS: Disciples, Thomas
SCRIPTURE: John 20:24-29
PROPS: blankets

All the disciples are together. See all the disciples sitting together. It is eight days after they first saw Jesus.

Now joining the disciples on the stage is Thomas. Watch as Thomas enters the room and does a sweet robot dance move!

Now watch as the disciples run to Thomas and begin moving their mouths up and down, and waving their arms around. They are telling Thomas that they saw Jesus. Jesus is alive!

But Thomas doesn't believe it. Watch as he shakes his head no and holds out his hand like a stop sign.

Watch as the disciples move their mouths up and down, and wave their arms around. They are telling Thomas that Jesus is alive! They saw him.

But Thomas still doesn't believe. See Thomas shake his head no and hold out his hand like a stop sign.

All of a sudden, Jesus is in the room. Watch as Jesus runs really fast into the room—and gives the disciples some fist bumps! Where did Jesus come from?

Jesus walks over to Thomas. Thomas has a big surprised face! Thomas is not sure what to believe and shakes his head.

See Jesus show Thomas his hands and feet. He still has nail marks from the cross.

Watch as Thomas looks carefully and thinks. Then Thomas gives everyone a big thumbs-up. Jesus is alive!

All the disciples give each other high-fives, and give fist bumps to Jesus.

Jesus is alive!

Great job, everyone. Let's cheer for our actors!

Discussion Questions
1. How do you think Thomas felt seeing Jesus?
2. How do you think you would feel seeing Jesus?

Breakfast With Jesus

CHARACTERS: Fishermen and Fisher-women, Jesus
SCRIPTURE: John 21:1-17
PROPS: paper fish, fishing nets (optional)

Now entering the room are some fishermen and fisher-women; watch as they give everyone a big wave hello!

These fisher-people are about to do some fishing. Watch as they cast their lines out and reel them back in. Then they do it again and again and again. Some fisher-people had nets. Watch as they try to catch the fish with a net. They have fished and fished and fished all night, and have caught nothing. Watch as they make big sad faces.

There is someone standing on the shore. Watch as the fisher-people point to the person. The person wants to know if they caught any fish. Watch as he moves his mouth up and down.

Watch as the fisher-people shout, "No!"

Now watch as the person moves his mouth up and down, and waves his arms around. It seems he is telling the fisher-people to try catching some fish one more time.

Watch as the fishermen and fisher-women try fishing one more time. Watch as they cast their lines out and reel them back in. All of sudden, they are catching some fish. Watch as some fish appear.

Just then, Simon Peter—one of the fishermen—recognizes the man on the shore as Jesus. Watch as Peter swims to Jesus and gives Jesus a high-five.

Soon, all the fisher-people join Jesus on shore. Jesus has made them all some breakfast. Watch as Jesus passes out the breakfast, and everyone rubs their stomachs.

Jesus wants to know how many fish they caught. Watch as everyone flashes a 1, a 5, and a 3 on their hands. They caught 153 fish.

Next, Jesus points to Peter. Listen as Jesus asks Peter: "Do you love me?" Listen as Peters says, "Yes."

Listen as Jesus asks Peter again: "Do you love me?" Peters answers, "Yes."

Listen as Jesus asks Peter one more time: "Do you love me?" Listen as Peter yells, "Yes."

Now watch as Jesus moves his mouth up and down, and waves his arms around. He is telling Peter to feed his sheep or tell everyone Peter can about Jesus. Watch as Jesus jumps up and gives Peter a high-five!

Great job, everyone. Let's cheer for our actors!

Discussion Questions
1. How do you think Peter felt with Jesus asking him questions?
2. How would you feel about Jesus asking you questions?

The Woman at the Well

CHARACTERS: Jesus, Woman, Disciples
SCRIPTURE: John 4:4-30
PROPS: bucket, water bottle

Now entering the room are Jesus and his disciples. Watch as Jesus waves to the crowd and the disciples do three jumping jacks.

Jesus and the disciples have been traveling all over town, teaching and healing people. Watch as Jesus moves his mouth up and down, and waves his arms around. He is telling the people all about God. Now watch as the disciples give Jesus a big thumbs-up. This is some good stuff, Jesus! This went on all day. Finally, Jesus points that way. Watch as Jesus points that way!

Jesus and the disciples are heading back to Galilee and to get there, they are going through—drumroll, please—Samaria! This makes the disciples scared! Watch as they make big scared faces. The disciples are also confused. Watch as the disciples make big confused faces. Why would Jesus take them through Samaria?

Time-out! Watch as Jesus and the disciples make a letter *T*.

The people of Samaria do not get along with the Jewish people. The disciples are Jewish, and they think the Samaritans are weird and not cool at all. In fact, they would rather walk an extra ten miles than go anywhere near a Samaritan village.

OK. Time-in! Watch as Jesus and his disciples begin walking into Samaria and sit down around a bucket. This is not a bucket, but a well where people get water.

Watch as the disciples begin to rub their bellies. They are getting pretty hungry. Watch as they make big hungry faces. Now watch as the disciples point to the door and move their mouths up and down, and wave their arms around. They are going to get food. Watch as they leave the room.

Now entering the room is a Samaritan woman. She slowly walks up to the bucket, I mean, well, and starts to fill her water bottle with water. Now watch as Jesus moves his mouth up and down, and waves his arms around. He is telling the Samaritan woman that he can offer her living water, in other words, God's love.

Watch as the Samaritan woman scratches her head and then makes a confused face. The Jewish people have said God's love is only for them and not for the Samaritans. Watch as Jesus shakes his head and stretches his arms out wide! Jesus is telling the Samaritan woman that God's love is big enough for everyone! This makes the Samaritan woman super excited! Watch as she gives Jesus a high-five, then jumps really high in the air! I mean, really high in the air!

Now the Samaritan woman leaves and goes out to tell everyone she can that Jesus is at the bucket, I mean, well, and that God loves the Samaritans too!

Great job, everyone. Let's cheer for our actors!

Discussion Questions
1. How do you think the Samaritan woman felt talking with Jesus?
2. How would you have felt hearing the Samaritan woman's story?

Disciples See Jesus

CHARACTERS: Disciples
SCRIPTURE: John 20:19-23
PROPS: blankets

This story takes place after Jesus rose from the dead. In fact, the Book of John says it was Easter night. Now entering the room are the disciples. Watch as the disciples wave to the crowd. It had been a long week for the disciples, and they were tired. Watch as they yawn big and stretch their arms way into the sky.

Not only are the disciples tired, but they are scared. Watch as they make big scared faces. They are scared because they think they are going to be in trouble. They are followers of Jesus. They haven't seen Jesus since he died on the cross. Watch as the disciples make a cross with their arms.

To stay safe, the disciples lock every door in the room. Watch as the disciples check each door in the room to be sure it is closed and locked. Finally, they bring out their safety blankies and wrap them around themselves. Now they are safe.

Now watch as the disciples sit down and look worried. What is going to happen?

All of a sudden, Jesus is in the room. Watch as Jesus runs really fast into the room, and gives the disciples some fist bumps! Where did Jesus come from?

Watch as the disciples stand up and begin inspecting Jesus. Is this really Jesus? Watch as they touch his head and his shoulder and his feet to be sure it is really him.

Now watch as Jesus moves his mouth up and down, and waves his arms around. Jesus is giving them a blessing.

Now watch as Jesus shows the disciples his feet and hands; there are still marks from the nails. Watch as the disciples stare at Jesus.

They realize it is really Jesus, and they are so happy! Watch as the disciples jump high in the sky! I mean, really high in the sky! I mean, really, really high in the sky!

Then Jesus waves goodbye and leaves the room.

Jesus is alive!

Great job, everyone. Let's cheer for our actors!

Discussion Questions
1. How do you think the disciples felt seeing Jesus?
2. How do you think the disciples felt after Jesus left?

Jesus Blesses Kids

CHARACTERS: Jesus, Disciples, Kids
SCRIPTURE: Mark 10:13-16
PROPS: none

Now entering the room is Jesus. Let's all cheer for Jesus!

Jesus is a busy guy. He heals a lot of people! He talks to a lot of people. Watch as he moves his mouth up and down, and waves his arms around. Jesus has messages of God's love for all the people.

Now entering the room are Jesus' disciples. Watch as they wave to the crowd and do three jumping jacks. The disciples like to take care of Jesus. Watch as they pat Jesus on the back, then give him high-fives!

One day Jesus is having a conversation with lots of people. Watch as he begins talking to the crowd.

The crowd, which is all of you sitting in the room, gives Jesus a big thumbs-up. You are loving what Jesus is telling you! The disciples think this is awesome too! Watch as they clap and give each other high-fives.

Now entering the room is a group of kids. Watch as they wave to the crowd, and then point to Jesus and give Jesus a big thumbs-up! They think Jesus is awesome and want to see him. Watch as the kids begin walking toward Jesus; they want to give Jesus high-fives.

The disciples notice the kids and quickly walk over to them. Watch as the disciples make big mean faces toward the kids and shake their heads no. Then the disciples point to the door.

The disciples move their mouths up and down, and wave their arms around. They are telling the kids that Jesus is a busy guy and does not have time for them; they need to go home and finish their homework.

Watch as the kids make big sad faces and begin walking toward the door. Poor kids.

Wait a minute! Jesus has stopped talking. Watch as he points to the disciples and nods his head yes!

Now watch as Jesus moves his mouth up and down, and waves his arms around. He is telling the disciples to bring the kids over. He always has time for the kids.

Watch as the kids turn around and make big smiley faces! They are so excited; they run to Jesus and give him a bunch of high-fives.

Watch as Jesus raises his arms in the air, then pats the kids on their heads. Jesus is glad to see the kids. He thinks kids are pretty important too.

Jesus says, "Allow the children to come to me. Don't forbid them, because God's kingdom belongs to people like these children."

Great job, everyone. Let's cheer for our actors!

Discussion Questions

1. How do you think the children felt seeing Jesus?
2. How would you feel seeing Jesus?

Water Into Wine

CHARACTERS: Partygoers, Servant, Jesus
SCRIPTURE: John 2:1-12
PROPS: good snacks on a tray, box, bottles of water, bag, bottles of soda

There was a wedding in Cana of Galilee, and the mother of Jesus was there. Jesus and his disciples were also invited to the wedding.

Welcome, everyone, to the wedding party! Watch as the partygoers enter the room waving to the crowd and smiling big! This has been an awesome party. This is actually day three of this most amazing wedding party. Watch as the partygoers each hold up three fingers.

One fun thing to do at a wedding party is eat all the good food. Watch as a servant enters the room with lots of snacks and hands them to our partygoers. Now watch as the partygoers smile big and give the servant high-fives. Great food!

Another important part of the wedding party is the dancing. Watch as all our partygoers start doing the robot. C'mon, partygoers, let's see the robot! Wow! Great dancing! After all that dancing, the partygoers are thirsty. Watch as they stick out their tongues and point at the servant.

Watch as the partygoers wave their arms around, and move their mouths up and down. They are telling the servant they are thirsty and want nice cold glasses of soda!

The servant nods his or her head and walks out of the room. After a few short moments, he or she returns to the room and hands the partygoers each a bottle of water from his or her box.

Watch as the partygoers make big confused faces. They don't want water. This is a party; they should have all the soda they want.

The servant shrugs her or his shoulders and begins moving her or his mouth up and down. She or he is telling the partygoers that all that is left is water, and the soda is all gone.

What kind of party is this where they run out of soda after only three days? Watch as the servant leaves the room.

Now entering the room is Jesus. Let's cheer for Jesus! Watch as Jesus waves to the servant and hands him or her the same box the servant was carrying out. Now watch as Jesus points to the crowd on stage and moves his mouth up and down.

Jesus is telling the servant to take the drinks back to the people; they will be happy with what is inside.

The servant walks over to the stage and opens the box, and inside there is soda! Wow! Watch as the servant makes a big surprised face and then waves to Jesus! Jesus has just performed an amazing miracle.

Now watch as the partygoers do the robot dance one more time! This wedding party is awesome!

Great job, everyone. Let's cheer for our actors!

Discussion Questions

1. How do you think Jesus felt when his mother told him to perform a miracle?
2. How would you have felt if you had seen the miracle?

Jesus Heals the Sick Servant

INSTANT DRAMA

CHARACTERS: Roman Officer, Servant, Friends
SCRIPTURE: Luke 7:1-10
PROPS: "Trust God" sign

Our story today is about someone who trusted God. Watch as a Roman officer enters the room. Let's make a siren sound to announce him!

The officer has a big problem; his young servant is home sick in bed. Watch as the servant enters the room. Listen as the servant begins to cough, then coughs some more, and then lies down on the floor.

Now watch as some friends enter the room looking very sad. Watch as they point to the sick servant and then make very sad faces. No matter how his friends try to help, the servant just gets sicker and sicker. Watch as his friends kneel around the young servant.

The Roman officer doesn't know what else to do. But then he remembers that no matter who you are, trust God! Watch as the servant's friends hold up a sign that reads, "Trust God."

So the Roman officer goes to see Jesus. Watch as the Roman officer waves goodbye to the friends and the sick servant, and begins walking around the room looking for Jesus.

Now entering the room is Jesus! Let's all cheer for Jesus. Watch as Jesus gives everyone a big thumbs-up.

Watch as the Roman officer runs over to Jesus and begins moving his mouth up and down, and waves his arms around. The Roman officer is begging Jesus to heal his young servant. Watch as the officer gets on his knees and begs.

Jesus replies, "I will come and heal him." Watch as all the friends clap and cheer.

But the officer shakes his head no, then says, "Lord, I am not worthy. Just say the word right here, and my servant will be healed." Watch as the officer kneels and bows his head.

When Jesus hears this, he is amazed. Watch as everyone makes big surprised faces!

Jesus says, "You have great faith! Go back home; your servant is healed." Watch as everyone points to the sick servant.

Now watch as the young servant stands up and gives everyone a thumbs-up! He is feeling great! Watch as the servant jumps really high in the air! I mean, really high in the air.

Everyone was so happy that Jesus healed their friend! Watch as the friends give out some high-fives!

Great job, everyone. Let's cheer for our actors!

Discussion Questions
1. How do you think the servant felt when he was healed?
2. How do you think the officer felt asking Jesus to heal the servant?

Zacchaeus

CHARACTERS: Zack, Friend 1, Friend 2, Jesus, Crowd
SCRIPTURE: Luke 19:1-10
PROPS: money: fake or real, chair

Zacchaeus, also known as Zack, is now entering the room. Watch as Zack walks in and waves to the crowd. Zack is a tax collector, which means he collects money from the people and gives it to the king.

Watch as Zack claps his hands and in walks Friend 1. Watch as Friend 1 waves to the crowd, then does five jumping jacks. Now watch as Zack holds out his hand and points to his friend. It is time to pay up! Watch as Friend 1 hands Zack some money, makes an angry face, then leaves the room.

Now watch as Zack claps his hands and in walks Friend 2. Watch as Friend 2 waves to the crowd, then does a sweet ninja move. See Zack hold out his hand and point at his friend. It is time to pay up! Watch as Friend 2 hands Zack some money, makes an angry face, then leaves the room.

This is what Zack does every day; this is his job. However, he often takes more money than he is supposed to and keeps the extra cash for himself. You see, Zack loves money! Watch as Zack hugs the money.

One day Jesus is passing through Zack's town. Watch as Jesus walks around the room with the crowd following him. Zack wants to get a good look at Jesus, but he is too short. So Zack decides to climb a tree, I mean, a chair, so he can look at Jesus and hear what Jesus has to say.

Watch as Jesus stops walking and begins moving his mouth up and down, and waving his arms around. Jesus is telling the crowd some great stuff. The crowd loves Jesus' message; watch as the crowd gives Jesus a big thumbs-up!

Now watch as Jesus points to Zack and says, "Come here!" Zack quickly gets off the chair and walks over to Jesus. Watch as Jesus waves his arms around, and moves his mouth up and down. He is talking to Zack, telling Zack about God's love for him.

The crowd is so surprised by Jesus talking to Zack; watch as everyone makes big surprised faces! Why would Jesus talk to someone who steals money from people? Jesus is telling Zack that God loves him and that he is going to have dinner with Zack!

After dinner, Zack is a changed dude! He decides he needs to start helping people instead of stealing from them. Watch as he begins handing out his money to the crowd.

From that day on, Zack followed Jesus and no longer stole money from people.

Great job, everyone. Let's cheer for our actors!

Discussion Questions
1. How do you think Zack felt, having Jesus come to his house for dinner?
2. How do you think you would feel if Jesus came to your house for dinner?

Lazarus

CHARACTERS: Lazarus, Mary, Martha, Jesus, Friends
SCRIPTURE: John 11:1-44
PROPS: two cell phones

Now entering the room is Lazarus. Let's cheer for Lazarus! Lazarus has two sisters: one named Mary, and one named Martha. Let's hold up two fingers as Lazarus' sisters join him.

Look over in the corner of the room where Jesus is waving to us. Jesus is good friends with Lazarus and his sisters. Let's watch as they give each other a big thumbs-up.

One day Lazarus gets sick. Watch as Lazarus touches his forehead, then his stomach. Now listen as Lazarus coughs and coughs again. Watch as Lazarus falls to the floor.

His sisters are worried about Lazarus. Watch as Mary and Martha run over to Lazarus and make big worried faces. Then the two sisters have a great idea. Watch as they point to their heads.

Martha and Mary will send a message to Jesus. Watch as Mary gets out her phone and sends a text to Jesus. Watch as Jesus pulls out his phone and reads the text.

Even though Jesus loves Lazarus, Mary, and Martha, he stays where he is. Watch as Jesus waves to everyone in the corner of the room.

Meanwhile, Lazarus gets sicker. Listen as Lazarus coughs and coughs again and coughs again! Mary and Martha are waiting for Jesus to come. Watch as they stand looking off in the distance. Lazarus gets sicker. Nothing his friends do makes him better. Watch as his friends come over to Lazarus and make big worried faces!

Mary, Martha, and their friends are waiting and watching for Jesus to come. Look at all of them standing, looking around with pretend binoculars.

Finally, Lazarus dies. Listen as Lazarus coughs one more time and then closes his eyes. Mary and Martha and the friends are very sad. Watch as they make big sad faces.

Finally, Jesus goes to see Mary and Martha. Watch as Jesus walks over to Mary and Martha. Watch as Mary and Martha move their mouths up and down, and wave their arms around. They are telling Jesus that if he had been here, Lazarus would not have died. Watch as everyone looks sad.

Watch as Jesus moves his mouth up and down, and waves his arms around. Jesus is telling everyone that he is the Son of God and has power over death, so just believe. Watch as Jesus prays to God and then shouts, "Lazarus, wake up!" Watch as Lazarus slowly stands up and looks around. Listen as Lazarus yells, "I feel great!"

Lazarus is alive! Watch as everyone jumps up and down, and waves their hands in the air.

Great job, everyone. Let's cheer for our actors!

Discussion Questions

1. How do you think Mary and Martha felt when Jesus did not come immediately to help Lazarus?
2. How do you think you would feel if you saw Jesus bring Lazarus back to life?

Lost Sheep

CHARACTERS: Shepherd, 1 Lost Sheep, Flock of Sheep
SCRIPTURE: Luke 15:1-7
PROPS: white hats for sheep

Now walking into the room is a cute little sheep. Watch as the sheep waves, then baas. Excuse me, Sheep, could you baa a little louder? Thank you, Sheep! This sheep is really good at tricks. Watch as it sits, does a jumping jack, and dances the robot. This sheep is really awesome!

This sheep also has a problem. It is lost. Watch as the sheep makes a big sad face. This sheep has 99 friends and somehow has gotten separated from all of them. Most importantly, this sheep has lost track of the shepherd. The sheep is really scared. Watch as the sheep makes a big scared face and looks around.

The sheep has decided to go hide so that it will stay safe. Watch as the sheep goes and hides. Now entering the room is the shepherd. Let's cheer for the shepherd! Watch as the shepherd gives everyone a big thumbs-up! This shepherd is so good!

Watch as the shepherd claps her or his hands three times, and in runs all the sheep. Look at all these sheep. Watch as the sheep give some high-fives and then show off their best ninja moves! Watch as the shepherd begins counting them. This could take a while.

...97, 98, 99. Yikes! The shepherd is missing one sheep. Watch as the shepherd makes a big surprised face and begins counting them again...97, 98, 99. Still one short!

Watch as the shepherd tells all the sheep to sit down and wait. The sheep are all confused. Watch as the sheep make big confused faces.

The shepherd leaves the sheep behind and begins looking all over the room for the one missing sheep. Watch as the shepherd looks out the window, out the door, and behind (insert name of leader in room), but there is no sheep. The shepherd is not giving up.

Watch as the shepherd looks in the trash can and then in the cabinet! Still no sign of the lost sheep. Hey, Shepherd, try looking again in the crowd! Watch as the shepherd looks carefully and finds the lost sheep!

The shepherd is so happy! Watch as the shepherd jumps high in the air. I mean, really high in the air! I mean, REALLY high in the air! Watch as the sheep and the shepherd give high-fives. Now watch as the shepherd leads the sheep back to the flock. Everyone is so happy!

Jesus told this story to show us how much God loves us.

Great job, everyone. Let's cheer for our actors!

Discussion Questions

1. How do you think the shepherd felt when one sheep was missing?

2. How do you think God feels when the lost are found?

Mary and Martha

CHARACTERS: Mary, Martha, Jesus, Messenger, Disciples
SCRIPTURE: Luke 10:38-42
PROPS: chair, bag of chips, bottle of water, banana

Standing at the front of the room are two sisters, Mary and Martha. Watch as they wave to the crowd, and give each other a fist bump. Mary and Martha are not only sisters, but they are best friends. They are such good friends that they live together in the same house.

A messenger comes over to Mary and Martha. Watch as the messenger does his best ninja move. The messenger moves his mouth up and down, and waves his arms around. He is telling Mary and Martha that Jesus will be stopping by in just a few minutes. Mary and Martha are so excited, they give the messenger high-fives. The messenger does one more ninja move, waves to the crowd, and then leaves.

A few minutes pass, and Jesus and his disciples arrive. Watch as Jesus enters the stage, shakes Mary's and Martha's hands, and then waves to the crowd. Next, Jesus points to his disciples and they enter the stage doing three jumping jacks.

Watch as Jesus yawns and rubs his feet; it has been a long day of traveling. Watch as he points to the chair and asks if he can sit down. Mary and Martha nod their heads yes, and Jesus sits down. Jesus begins moving his mouth up and down, and waves his arms around. He's telling everyone some good stuff. Watch as everyone gives Jesus a thumbs-up.

Mary and the disciples sit around Jesus and begin listening. Watch as they pull on their ears and yell, "More stories, Jesus!" Jesus continues moving his mouth up and down, and waving his arms around. He's telling everyone some good stuff. Watch as everyone gives Jesus a thumbs-up.

Now watch as Martha realizes it's almost lunchtime, and she doesn't have anything ready for lunch. Watch as she runs to the side of the stage and begins getting some lunch ready. Watch as Martha pulls out a bag of chips and a banana, and brings them over to Jesus. Listen as Jesus says thank you. Then Martha realizes Jesus must be thirsty. Watch as she runs back to her kitchen and gets a bottle of water. Watch as Martha runs the water over to Jesus and listen as Jesus says thank you.

Now watch as Martha makes a big angry face at Mary! Why isn't she helping serve the guests? Watch as Martha taps on Jesus' shoulder and begins moving her mouth up and down, and waving her arms around. She is not very happy with Mary. She's been doing all the work, while Mary has been sitting around.

Watch as Jesus smiles and stands up. Watch as Jesus gives Mary a big thumbs-up. Jesus wishes Martha had spent time listening to Jesus, instead of being so busy getting Jesus food.

Watch as everyone stands up, scratches his or her head, and then gives Jesus a thumbs-up. They will be sure to spend more time with Jesus from now on.

Great job, everyone. Let's cheer for our actors!

Discussion Questions
1. How do you think Mary felt listening to Jesus?
2. How do think you would feel if you were Martha?

The Sower

CHARACTERS: Farmer, Kids, Birds, Sun, Thorns, Healthy Plants
SCRIPTURE: Matthew 13:1-9
PROPS: straw hat, paper bag of seeds, yellow circle, green branches

One day Jesus told this story to the people.

A farmer went out to plant seeds. Watch as the farmer skips into the room carrying a bag of seeds. See the farmer wave to everyone in the crowd and even give a few people a high-five! The farmer loves planting season. Watch as the farmer smiles big and gives everyone a big thumbs-up.

The farmer begins tossing the seeds onto the ground; watch as the farmer throws the seeds. Some of the seeds fall on a walking path. Watch as some kids enter the room and walk all over the seeds. Now watch as a couple of birds fly in the room and begin eating the seeds. Watch as the birds and the kids exit the room. Poor farmer; these seeds will not grow at all. Watch as the farmer makes a big sad face.

No worries; the farmer has more seeds! Watch as the farmer tosses out more seeds. Some of these seeds fall on rocky soil. Now watch as the sun enters the room. The seeds on the rocky soil only grow a little bit because there is not enough water, and the sun is so hot. Watch as the sun flexes its muscles! Now watch as the sun exits the room. Poor farmer; these seeds do not grow very well at all. Watch as the farmer makes a big sad face.

But no worries—the farmer has more seeds! Watch as the farmer tosses out more seeds. Some of these seeds fall on thorny soil. Watch as the thorns enter the room and make some big muscles! Wow! These thorns look pretty scary. The seeds that are on the thorny soil only grow a little bit before the thorns steal all the water and sunshine.

Watch as the thorns grab some of the seeds from the floor and exit the room. Poor farmer; these seeds do not grow very well at all. Watch as the farmer makes a big sad face.

Watch as the farmer tosses out more seeds. These seeds fall on the good soil. Watch as some beautiful-looking plants enter the room. See how happy they are. These plants get the right amount of water and sun, but most importantly, they were planted in the right soil. Watch as the farmer and the plants give each other some high-fives.

Jesus told this story and said the seeds are like the stories of the Bible we hear at church or read in the Bible, and we are like the soil. When we hear the stories of the Bible, we are good soil.

Great job, everyone. Let's cheer for our actors!

Discussion Questions
1. How do you think it would feel to be the good soil?
2. How do you feel hearing our story today?

The Talents

CHARACTERS: Boss, 3 Workers, Crowd
SCRIPTURE: Matthew 25:14-30
PROPS: money: real or fake

Now entering the room is the boss. See how important the boss is! See the boss cross his or her arms and make a big mean face! Yikes!

Now watch as the workers enter the room, skipping. They are so happy and love their jobs! Watch as the boss hands each of the workers some money. The first worker gets ten dollars, the second worker gets five dollars, and the third worker gets one dollar. Now watch as the boss waves goodbye. He or she is going on a vacation and wants the workers to make good use of the money.

The worker with ten dollars scratches her or his head and then points to the sky. The worker has an idea. Watch as the worker leaves the room.

Watch as the worker with five dollars scratches his or her head and then points to the sky. The worker has an idea. Watch the worker leave the room.

Now the worker with one dollar has an idea. This worker decides to hide the money in the corner of the room to keep it safe. Watch as the worker walks to the corner of the room and hides the money. Not sure that this is a great idea.

Time passes; watch as the crowd looks at their watches and then at the clock on the wall, and then yells, "Ticktock, ticktock!"

Finally, the boss returns from vacation and is excited to be back. Watch as the boss claps his or her hands and all the workers return with their money.

Watch the first worker hand the boss not ten dollars, but twenty dollars. This makes the boss happy; watch as they give each other a really big high-ten. This worker did a great job.

Now the second worker hands the boss not five dollars, but ten dollars! This makes the boss super-pumped. Watch as the boss gives the worker a fist bump. This worker did a great job.

Finally, the third worker hands the boss one dollar. The boss is not too happy. Watch as he or she waves his or her arms around, and moves his or her mouth up and down. The boss wishes the worker would have done something with the money. Watch as the boss makes a big sad face. Watch as the worker looks sad and then leaves the room.

Jesus told this story called a parable to remind us that God has given each of us gifts and talents. It may not be money, but something we are good at doing. Whatever it is, we need to use these gifts to help others know more about Jesus.

Great job, everyone. Let's cheer for our actors!

Discussion Questions
1. How do you think it felt to receive the ten dollars?
2. How would you feel if you had brought more money back to the boss?

The Vineyard

CHARACTERS: Boss, 3 Sets of Workers
SCRIPTURE: Matthew 20:1-16
PROPS: picture of a field, money: fake or real

Now entering the room is the boss. Watch as the boss does a few jumping jacks. The boss is ready to start the day. The boss owns a lot of land! Watch as the boss points to a picture of the land. Wow, that is a pretty nice patch of land!

On the boss's land are some grapes that need to be harvested, and the boss does not have time to do it. Watch as the boss claps and in walks a few workers. These workers are looking to make some cash today. Watch as the boss waves his or her arms around, and moves his or her mouth up down. Now watch as the workers move their mouths up and down, and wave their arms around. Now watch as they shake hands.

The boss and the workers have agreed that if the workers work all day long picking grapes, they will make one million dollars. Wait—not that much; probably more like fifty bucks, but still pretty good.

Watch as the boss leaves and the workers begin walking around picking grapes.

Watch as they reach up high to pick grapes, then reach down low to pick grapes, then back up high. They are very good at picking grapes.

It's about lunchtime, and the boss returns with a few more workers. Watch as the workers and the boss shake hands. Now watch as the boss leaves and all the workers get back to work.

Watch as they reach up high to pick grapes, then reach down low to pick grapes, then back up high. They are very good at picking grapes.

It's near the end of the day, and the boss returns with more workers. Watch as the workers and the boss shake hands. Now watch as the boss leaves and all the workers get back to work.

Watch as they reach up high to pick grapes, then reach down low to pick grapes, then back up high. They are very good at picking grapes.

Beep, beep, beep. It's quitting time after a long day of work. Watch as the boss returns and begins handing out money to all the workers.

Every worker is given fifty bucks, just like the boss promised. But the workers who have worked all day are confused. Watch as they make big confused faces. Why did the workers who worked only a few short minutes get the same as those who worked all day?

Watch as the boss waves his or her arms around, and moves his or her mouth up and down. The boss is telling the workers that he or she is keeping his or her word to everyone, and why should they be worried if the boss wants to be nice and generous?

Jesus told this story to remind the people that God is always fair and always generous with love and kindness toward us.

Great job, everyone. Let's cheer for our actors!

Discussion Questions
1. How do you think it felt to be the workers who worked the least amount of time?
2. How would you have felt if you had worked the most amount of time?

The Rich Farmer

CHARACTERS: Farmer Jane, 2–3 Small Barns, 2–3 Big Barns
SCRIPTURE: Luke 12:13-21
PROPS: baskets of fruit or vegetables

Standing in front of you now is Farmer Jane! She is a nice farmer. Watch as she smiles big and then does a ninja move. Farmer Jane has been a farmer for many years! She is very good at farming; watch as she gives everyone a big thumbs-up.

Standing next to Farmer Jane are some of her really awesome small barns. Watch as the barns bow and then flex their muscles. As you can see, these barns are really awesome at holding a bunch of the crops Farmer Jane has harvested. Watch as the barns show off some of the cool stuff in their baskets.

Now watch as Farmer Jane starts working the field. Watch as she drives the tractor around the stage. Now watch as she rakes the field. Now watch as she does the sprinkler dance move and waters the fields.

Farmer Jane is going to have a problem. Watch as she stands next to her barns and begins walking around them and looking at them. The barns look worried; watch as they make big scared faces! What is Farmer Jane doing?

These barns are too small; watch as Farmer Jane shakes her head no. These barns have to go.

Watch as Farmer Jane lightly pushes on the barns. Watch as the barns wave goodbye and fall over. Goodbye, barns; we will miss you. Now what is Farmer Jane doing? Watch as she claps her hands and in walks some really big barns.

These barns are totally awesome; watch as they flex their muscles and wave to the crowd. These barns can really hold a lot of stuff.

Now watch as Farmer Jane starts working the field. Watch as she drives the tractor around the stage. Now watch as she rakes the field. Now watch as she does the sprinkler and waters the fields. Farmer Jane, shouldn't you take a break from all this farming? Watch as Farmer Jane shakes her head no.

It seems to me that all Farmer Jane cares about is her barns and nothing else. This make God very sad.

Jesus told this story to remind us that God should be number one in our lives—not farming, video games, sports, dance troupes, or anything else.

That night, Farmer Jane got in a little bit of trouble for only caring about her barns and nothing else. Listen as Jane yells, "Uh-oh," and then leaves the room.

Great job, everyone. Let's cheer for our actors!

Discussion Questions
1. How do you think Farmer Jane felt when she needed bigger barns?
2. How do you feel about making God number one?

Paul's Adventures

CHARACTERS: Paul, Mean People, Mean Dude, Shortest Person in the Room, Waves, Police Officer, Snake

SCRIPTURE: Acts 9; 21; 27

PROPS: socks, basket, squirt gun

Now entering the room is Paul. Watch as Paul waves to the crowd and then shows off his best dance moves! Paul is a follower of Jesus. Watch as he points to the sky. Paul has a thankful heart. See Paul say thank you!

Paul has had some tough stuff happen in his life.

One day Paul is talking to everyone about Jesus. Watch as he waves his hands around, and moves his mouth up and down. Now entering the stage are some people who don't like Paul and his talking about Jesus. Watch as the mean people make big mean faces and throw some socks at him. Now watch as the mean people leave the room. But Paul didn't get angry, and he didn't give up! Listen as Paul says, "I'll keep following Jesus!"

Another time Paul is telling others about Jesus. Watch as he waves his arms around, and moves his mouth up and down. Now coming back into the room are the mean people; watch as they make mean faces and pound their fists into their hands. Now watch as they wave their arms around, and move their mouths up and down. They are telling Paul that as soon as he is done teaching, they are going to beat him up. They will be waiting for him outside. Watch as the mean dudes leave the room. But Paul didn't get angry, and he didn't give up! Listen as Paul says, "I'll keep following Jesus!"

Watch as a kid enters the room with a basket and hands it to Paul. Now watch as he moves his mouth up and down, and waves his arms around. He is telling Paul to get in the basket, and they will lower him out the window to safety. Paul is a little confused; see his big confused face. Paul says thank you! Paul has a big smile on his face.

Next, Paul is on a ship when all of a sudden, a big storm comes up. Watch as the waves get really big and make Paul all wet. The storm is so big, the boat crashes and Paul is left on an island. But Paul didn't get angry, and he didn't give up! Listen as Paul says, "I'll keep following Jesus!"

While on the island, Paul was bitten by a snake; watch as a snake enters the room and bites Paul. But Paul didn't get angry, and he didn't give up! Listen as Paul says, "I'll keep following Jesus!"

When Paul finally made it off the island, he was put in jail for telling others about Jesus. Watch as a police officer enters the room and ties Paul's hands around his back. But Paul didn't get angry, and he didn't give up! Listen as Paul says, "I'll keep following Jesus!"

Finally, Paul spent many months in jail for following Jesus, but Paul kept smiling big and telling everyone to follow Jesus.

Great job, everyone. Let's cheer for our actors!

Discussion Questions
1. How do you think Paul felt, talking about Jesus?
2. How do you feel, talking about Jesus?

Ten Lepers

INSTANT DRAMA

CHARACTERS: 10 Lepers (assign one to be the Thankful Leper), Jesus
SCRIPTURE: Luke 17:11-19
PROPS: none

Now entering the room are some very sick lepers. Watch as the lepers make big sad faces and wave to everyone in the audience.

These lepers have been sick for a very, very, very long time. Watch as they cough, scratch their arms, scratch their legs, then cough again.

Being a leper is no fun. Watch as they give everyone a big thumbs-down.

Lepers have a terrible skin disease which makes them itchy; watch as they scratch their arms and legs.

It is also quite painful to be a leper; watch as the lepers yell in pain.

These lepers cannot spend any time at home, which makes them sad; watch as they make big sad faces.

Poor lepers; they have been sick for a long time. Watch as they lift their arms to the sky and ask God for healing.

One day a visitor happens to be walking near the lepers. Watch as the visitor now enters the room and waves to everyone.

This is no ordinary visitor; it is Jesus!

The lepers had heard all about Jesus! Watch as they walk up to Jesus and point to their arms, their legs, and their feet. Now watch as they begin scratching their legs and arms.

Now watch as the lepers move their mouths up and down, and wave their arms around. They are asking Jesus to heal them and get rid of their leprosy.

Watch as Jesus nods his head yes, then points to the sky, and then points at the lepers.

All of a sudden, the lepers begin feeling awesome again! Their sickness is gone. Watch as they jump up and down, and give each other high-fives.

The lepers are so excited to go tell their families and friends; watch as they run out of the room.

Now watch as one of the lepers walks back into the room and walks over to Jesus.

Watch as the leper says, "Thank you, Jesus!"

Great job, everyone. Let's cheer for our actors!

Discussion Questions
1. How do you think Jesus felt when the one leper said thank you?
2. How do you feel when you say thank you?

Blind Bart

CHARACTERS: Jesus, Bart, Friend 1, Friend 2, Friend 3
SCRIPTURE: Mark 10:46-52
PROPS: bucket, fake money

Sitting before us now is Blind Bart; watch as Bart waves and holds out his bucket. Bart is blind, which means he cannot see. Watch as Bart points to his eyes.

Every day Bart sits at the side of the road and begs for money. He uses this money to buy food.

Watch as Friend 1 enters the room, skipping! She or he is having a terrific day! Listen as Bart yells, "Help me!" and holds up his bucket. See Friend 1 toss a coin into the bucket and then skip out of the room.

Watch as Friend 2 enters the room, hopping! He or she is having a terrific day! Listen as Bart yells, "Help me!" and holds up his bucket. Watch as Friend 2 tosses a coin into the bucket and then hops out of the room.

Watch as Friend 3 enters the room, waving to everyone! She or he is having a terrific day! Listen as Bart yells, "Help me!" and holds up his bucket. Watch as Friend 3 tosses a coin into the bucket and then waves all the way out of the room.

This is how Blind Bart's day is every day—all the time, every week, every month, every year—until one day!

Now entering the room is Jesus. Let's cheer for Jesus! Watch as Jesus waves to the crowd and gives everyone a big thumbs-up.

Watch as Bart stands up. Listen as Bart yells, "Help me!" and holds up his bucket.

Jesus walks over to Bart and shakes Bart's hand. Jesus cares about Bart a bunch. Jesus is going to do something amazing! Are you ready?

Watch as Jesus points to Bart's eyes and then taps Bart on the shoulders.

All of a sudden, Bart's eyes are open. Bart can see. Bart is so happy! Watch as Bart smiles big and jumps high in the air. I mean, really high in the air, and then gives Jesus a fist bump.

Listen as Bart yells, "Thank you, Jesus!" Watch as Jesus gives Bart a thumbs-up and heads out of the room.

But wait—Bart is not staying here anymore. Bart is going to follow Jesus; watch as Bart runs out of the room to catch up with Jesus.

In this story, Jesus heals Bart, and Bart follows Jesus.

Great job, everyone. Let's cheer for our actors!

Discussion Questions
1. How do you think Bart felt having to ask for help every day?
2. How do you think Bart felt when Jesus healed him?

Caring for Others

CHARACTERS: Jesus, Cold Person, Hungry Person, Sick Person, Thirsty Person, Sad Person
SCRIPTURE: Matthew 25:35-40
PROPS: coat, snack, juice box, cough drops

Now entering the room is Jesus. Let's all cheer for Jesus!

Jesus has an important message to share with us. Watch as he moves his mouth up and down, and waves his arms around. Now watch as Jesus points to the door.

Now entering the room is a very cold person. Watch as he or she shivers and gives himself or herself a big hug. He or she is so cold! Jesus looks at the cold person and then hands the person the coat he was wearing. Wow! That is very caring, Jesus. Watch as the cold person smiles big, gives Jesus a high-five, and then leaves the room.

Now entering the room is a very hungry person; watch as she or he rubs her or his stomach and looks around the room for food. Now watch as she or he rubs her or his belly again. Jesus looks at the hungry person and then hands her or him a few snacks. Wow! That is very caring, Jesus! Watch as the hungry person smiles big, gives Jesus a high-five, and then leaves the room.

Now entering the room is a very sick person; watch as he or she pretends to cough and cough some more and cough a little bit more. Jesus looks at the sick person and hands him or her a couple of cough drops! Wow! That is very caring, Jesus! Watch as the sick person smiles big, gives Jesus a high-five, and then leaves the room.

Now watch as a very thirsty person enters the room. Watch as she or he sticks out her or his tongue. She or he is so thirsty. She or he is looking everywhere for a water fountain. Jesus sees the thirsty person and gives the person his very last juice box! So nice, Jesus! Watch as the thirsty person jumps up and down, gives Jesus a high-five, and then leaves the room.

Finally, watch as a very sad person enters the room. See that big sad face. This person doesn't really have any friends. Watch as Jesus sees the sad person and gives the sad person a handshake, a high-five, and a fist bump! Jesus is super nice!

Now watch as Jesus moves his mouth up and down, and begins waving his arms around. Jesus has one more very important thing to say. Watch as Jesus points to everyone in the crowd. Jesus wants us to do the same things he just did—care for those in need, be friends to those without any friends, and give to others if they are hungry or thirsty.

Now watch as Jesus and his new friend give each other a high-five and exit the room. Let's remember that in this story, Jesus cares for those in need and we should also.

Great job, everyone. Let's cheer for our actors!

Discussion Questions
1. How do you think it feels to be cold, hungry, sick, or thirsty?
2. How do you feel about Jesus helping all these people?

Christmas

CHARACTERS: Mary, Joseph, Angel, Nice Persons 1 & 2, Innkeeper
SCRIPTURE: Luke 2
PROPS: wagon, stuffed animals, manger, baby doll

An angel appeared to both Mary and Joseph. Let's cheer loudly as Mary and Joseph enter the room! Watch as Mary and Joseph bow and wave to the crowd.

Now watch as an angel flies into the room. Well, maybe our angel just walks in. Watch as the angel waves his or her arms around, and moves his or her mouth up and down. The angel is telling Mary and Joseph that they are going to have a baby, and that baby is Jesus!

Watch as Mary and Joseph make big surprised faces, then scared faces, and then give the angel high-fives. Once they realize this is God keeping God's promise, they are cool! Then the angel goes away! Hear the angel say, "Adios, amigos," and wave goodbye.

The Roman Emperor declared that everyone needed to go to his hometown for taxes. This means Mary and Joseph have to travel to Bethlehem because Joseph is from King David's family in Bethlehem. Watch as Mary and Joseph begin to walk around the room. Actually, we think Mary rode a donkey. Watch as a donkey (wagon) enters the room; Mary gets a ride.

The trip to Bethlehem is eighty miles, and it takes a long time—probably over a week. But Mary and Joseph keep going, day after day, up the hill and down the hill.

Finally, Mary and Joseph make it to Bethlehem. Watch as Mary and Joseph make their way to the front of the room. When they arrive, Mary gets worried. Watch as she makes a big worried face. Now watch as she pats her belly. The baby is coming. She needs a place to lie down.

Watch as Joseph makes a big scared face! What to do? Watch as Joseph runs over to a door and knocks. Watch as Nice Person 1 opens the door and waves.

Listen as Joseph yells, "Do you have any room?" Listen as the nice person yells, "Sorry, not today!"

Now watch as Joseph runs to another door and knocks. Watch as Nice Person 2 opens the door and waves. Hear Joseph yell, "Do you have any room?" Hear the nice person yell, "Sorry, not today!"

Now watch as Joseph runs back on stage and gives Mary a big thumbs-down. He can't find anyplace for them to stay. Watch as Mary and Joseph make big sad faces. Now watch as an innkeeper walks in with a manger and some animals. Watch as he points all around and says, "You can stay here!" The innkeeper is offering his stable for the night, a place where he keeps his animals. Watch as Mary and Joseph look around and then give the innkeeper fist bumps and yell, "Thank you!"

That night baby Jesus is born and placed in a manger. Watch as baby Jesus enters the room and Mary puts him in the manger.

Great job, everyone. Let's cheer for our actors!

Discussion Questions
1. How do you think Mary and Joseph felt when they were visited by the angel?
2. How do you feel hearing our story today?

God's Gifts

CHARACTERS: 5 Contestants
SCRIPTURE: 1 Corinthians 12
PROPS: five gift boxes, each with one of the following: three small balls, paper, jump rope, robot picture and music, index card with two jokes written on it

NOTE: Make sure each contestant can do the talent, or change the talents according to the child.

Good evening, ladies and gentlemen, and welcome to tonight's show, "Kids Have Talent." Let's give a hand for our five contestants now entering the room! You'll notice that each contestant has a lovely wrapped gift. Each will open the gift and discover a hidden talent.

Let's start with Contestant 1; watch as she or he waves and opens the box. Go ahead, Contestant 1. Let's see what's inside. Wow! It's three juggling balls! I had no idea Contestant 1 could juggle! Go ahead and juggle for us. Great job, Contestant 1; what a gift you've got.

Now on to Contestant 2. Go ahead and open your gift! Wow! It's a piece of paper. I had no idea our contestant could fold paper into any animal we like. I say we go with a giraffe. Contestant 2, go ahead and make a giraffe! While you are working on that, we'll go to Contestant 3.

OK, Contestant 3, open your gift! Wow! Would you take a look at that; it's a jump rope. Did you know Contestant 3 can jump rope really fast! This is going to be great! Let's go, Contestant 3.

Nicely done! What talent you have. Wait, let's go back to Contestant 2 and see how that giraffe is coming. That is one nice-looking giraffe. Let's cheer for our contestants so far! They have some great gifts.

Now let's move to Contestant 4. Wow! Take a look; it's a robot. Did you know that Contestant 4 can do an amazing robot dance? Let's get some music going and see the robot dance!

Super awesome! Let's cheer for Contestant 4. Finally, we are on to Contestant 5. Go ahead, Contestant 5; you know what to do. Take a look inside, and there are some index cards. Did you know Contestant 5 is a comedian? Let's take a minute to listen to a couple of jokes.

Wow! What an amazing group of kids. God has made us all different and has given us different gifts. The Book of Corinthians tells us about the different gifts God gives us, and one gift is not better than another. All these gifts should be used to help people know more about God!

So let's give a hand to all our contestants one more time; thanks for playing!

Discussion Questions
1. How do you feel about God giving all of us talents to use?
2. How do you think you can help others discover their talents?

The Good Samaritan

INSTANT DRAMA

CHARACTERS: Jewish Man, Robbers, Temple Priest, Temple Assistant, Samaritan
SCRIPTURE: Luke 10:25-37
PROPS: money, shoes, hat, adhesive bandage, water bottle, bag

---

One day while Jesus was teaching about loving our neighbors, a man asked Jesus to explain something. The man wanted to know who our neighbors actually are. Did Jesus mean our next-door neighbors? People in our Lego® clubs? People who sit next to us at school? People who aren't even nice to us? Jesus answered by telling a story.

Now entering the room is a Jewish man. Watch as he waves and then begins walking around. Listen as he whistles while he walks.

Entering the room are some robbers! Watch as they flex their muscles and make some mean faces. What is this crew up to? Watch as the robbers walk over to the Jewish man. See the robbers take the man's money, shoes, and hat, then place him nicely on the ground. He is hurt pretty badly. The robbers leave, making big mean faces. The crowd gives the robbers a big thumbs-down!

Soon a temple priest walks by the Jewish man. The temple priest is the one waving to us right now. Watch as the temple priest stops and looks at the hurt man, but then steps over the hurt man and quickly heads out the door.

Later, a temple assistant walks by. He is smiling big and skipping around the room. Watch as he sees the hurt man on the ground. He stops and looks at the man, then continues skipping his way out the door.

Next, a Samaritan comes along. The Samaritan gives everyone a big thumbs-up! Nice! Samaritans and Jews do not like each other; watch as the Samaritan gives a thumbs-down.

The Samaritan stops next to the injured man and looks at him. He reaches into his bag and pulls out an adhesive bandage. Watch as the Samaritan puts the bandage on the Jewish man's head. Then the Samaritan gives the Jewish man water from his own water bottle. What a nice guy. The Samaritan helps the man up and carries him off to a hotel where he can get some more rest.

At the end of the story, Jesus asks who is the neighbor in this story. Everyone says the Samaritan. Jesus says, "Go and do likewise."

Great job, everyone. Let's cheer for our actors!

Discussion Questions

1. How do you think the Samaritan man felt helping the Jewish man?

2. How do you feel when the others stepped around the injured man?

Jesus Is Arrested

CHARACTERS: Religious Leaders, Jesus, Jesus' Disciples
SCRIPTURE: John 18
PROPS: none

Now entering the room are some religious leaders; watch as they frown and give everyone a big thumbs-down! The religious leaders are mad at Jesus and want to get rid of him. Watch as they huddle together and whisper to each other. Now watch as the leaders exit the room.

One night Jesus and his disciples go to a garden. Watch as Jesus and his friends enter the room.

Jesus tells his friends to wait at the doors while he prays to God. Watch as Jesus walks to the center of the room to kneel and pray.

Then Jesus and the disciples hear a loud noise, the sound of marching footsteps. Someone is coming. Watch as the religious leaders march into the room.

The leaders arrest Jesus, even though he had never done anything wrong. Watch as the leaders put Jesus' hands behind his back.

Now watch as the leaders point at Jesus and make angry faces.

The leaders are lying about Jesus. They are making up all sorts of things about Jesus.

But does Jesus get mad about this? Watch as Jesus shakes his head no. Does Jesus yell at the leaders? Watch as Jesus shakes his head no.

Instead, watch as Jesus bows his head and prays. Jesus is trusting God, even when bad stuff is happening.

Watch as Jesus points to the sky and then points to everyone in the room.

Jesus wants to remind us that no matter what happens to us, we should trust God.

Great job, everyone. Let's cheer for our actors!

Discussion Questions
1. How do you feel hearing that Jesus was arrested?
2. How do you think God felt that Jesus was arrested?

Peter Denies Jesus

CHARACTERS: Peter, Crowd, Lame Man, 3 People, Rooster
SCRIPTURE: Luke 22:54-62
PROPS: none

Our story is about Peter. Let's watch as Peter enters the room and waves to everyone! Peter is a follower of Jesus; watch as Peter points to the sky, then gives everyone a big thumbs-up. Peter thinks Jesus is pretty cool.

After Jesus was arrested, Peter follows Jesus to the palace. Peter is warming his hands by a fire in the courtyard. Watch as Peter rubs his hands together.

Now watch as another person comes to the fire and begins moving his or her mouth up and down, and pointing to the sky. This person is asking Peter if he knows Jesus. Now watch as Peter shakes his head no. Wait a minute; Peter knows Jesus! Why is he saying no?

Now watch as another person comes to the fire and begins moving her or his mouth up and down, and pointing to the sky. This person is asking Peter if he knows Jesus. Now watch as Peter shakes his head no.

Wait a minute; Peter knows Jesus! Why is he saying no again?

Now watch as Peter moves across the room to lean against a wall. Another person comes to Peter and begins moving his or her mouth up and down, and pointing to the sky. This person is asking Peter if he knows Jesus.

Now watch as Peter shakes his head no.

Wait a minute; Peter knows Jesus! Why is he saying no again?

Peter made a big mistake telling everyone he did not know Jesus when he really did. Watch as Peter makes a big sad face!

Peter remembers that Jesus told him he would deny Jesus three times before the rooster crowed. Listen as the rooster crows.

Peter feels really bad about denying Jesus. He is sorry, but Jesus forgives him. Now watch as Peter smiles big.

Good job, everyone. Let's cheer for our actors!

Discussion Questions

1. How do you think Peter felt after he had denied knowing Jesus?

2. How would you feel about being in the courtyard after Jesus was arrested?

Jailbreak

INSTANT DRAMA

CHARACTERS: King Herod, Peter, Soldiers, Angel
SCRIPTURE: Acts 12:1-14
PROPS: crown, chair, kazoo

Now entering the room to sit on his throne with his crown is King Herod. Let's all cheer for Herod! Actually, don't cheer for Herod. He is a mean dude! Watch as he makes a big mean face then gives everyone a big thumbs-down. Herod made fun of people who followed Jesus. Watch as he points to the crowd and begins laughing!

Not only did he make fun of people who followed Jesus; he put people in jail for following Jesus. This makes Herod happy; see him give everyone a big thumbs-up. Listen as Herod yells, "I am the king!"

Now entering at the back of the room is Peter. Watch as Peter waves to the crowd then does his best ninja move. Peter loves Jesus and tells everyone he can about Jesus. Watch as Peter points to the sky.

See Peter skip to the front and begin talking about Jesus. Watch as Peter moves his mouth up and down, and waves his arms around.

This makes Herod mad; watch as he makes a really mean face, then yells, "I am the king!" But Peter keeps talking about Jesus. Watch as Peter points to the sky, then moves his mouth up and down.

Listen as King Herod blows his kazoo and in walks some soldiers. These soldiers are some pretty tough dudes. Watch as they do two pushups and then two jumping jacks. Now watch as Herod points to Peter and yells, "Arrest this dude!"

The soldiers run over to Peter and tie up his hands, then take him to jail. The guards are also going to block the door, so no one can escape.

Herod is so happy; watch as he leaves the room and waves to the crowd. He's off to get some delicious burritos.

Soon people hear that Peter is in jail, and this makes them sad. Watch as the crowd, which is all of you, folds their hands and bows their heads. The church is praying for Peter! The crowd prays and prays and prays some more. God hears the people's prayer.

Watch as an angel comes flying into the room. OK, so our angel is just going to walk. Watch as the angel quietly walks over to Peter and wakes him up. Peter is so surprised! Look at Peter's big surprised face!

The angel tells Peter to be quiet and leads him out of the jail. Peter is so happy; watch as he jumps really high in the air.

The angel brings Peter to the crowd. They are so happy too. See the crowd give Peter a big thumbs-up! Next, everyone in the room points to the sky! They know God heard their prayers and answered in a big way.

Thank you, God, for hearing our prayers and saving Peter!

Great job, everyone. Let's cheer for our actors.

Discussion Questions

1. How do you think Peter felt when the angel opened the door to the jail?

2. How would you have felt seeing Peter out of jail?

On the Road Again

CHARACTERS: Philip, Cool Dude, Totally Awesome Dude, Coolest Person in the World, Angel, Ethiopian
SCRIPTURE: Acts 8:26-40
PROPS: Bible, angel costume (optional)

Meet Philip; he is the guy walking around the room and waving. Philip is a follower of Jesus, and he has been spreading the good news of Jesus' love to everyone!

Watch as Philip walks over to a cool dude and says, "Jesus loves you!" Now watch as Philip and the cool dude shake hands.

Watch as Philip walks over to a totally awesome dude and sings, "Jesus loves you!" Now watch as Philip and the totally awesome dude shake hands.

Watch as Philip walks over to the coolest person in the world and yells, "Jesus loves you!" Now watch as Philip and the coolest person in the world shake hands.

One day an angel appears to Philip. Watch as the angel flies into the room. Watch as the angel points to the sky. The angel has a message from God.

Watch as the angel points to an Ethiopian sitting over in the corner reading the Bible. The angel moves his or her mouth up and down, and waves his or her arms around. The angel is telling Philip to go over to the Ethiopian and tell him or her that Jesus loves him or her too. Watch as Philip nods his heads yes, and the angel disappears.

Now watch Philip run over to the Ethiopian and shake her or his hand. Watch as Philip points to the Bible and asks the Ethiopian if she or he understands the Bible. See the Ethiopian make a big confused face and shake her or his head no. The Ethiopian does not understand what the Bible is saying. Does Jesus love her or him too?

Watch as Philip moves his mouth up and down, and waves his arms around. He is telling the Ethiopian that Jesus' love is for everyone, and that Jesus loves him or her too.

This makes the Ethiopian happy; watch as she or he stands up and gives Philip a high-five! She or he is so pumped to have a new friend and even more excited to know that Jesus loves her or him too!

Now watch as both Philip and the Ethiopian get on their knees and pray. God's love brings people together. It unites us!

Great job, everyone. Let's cheer for our actors!

Discussion Questions
1. How do you think the Ethiopian felt meeting Philip?
2. How would you have felt if an angel visited you?

The Prodigal Son

CHARACTERS: Younger Son, Older Son, Dad, Salesperson, Chef
SCRIPTURE: Luke 15:11-32
PROPS: fake money, random object, bag of snacks

Now entering the room are two sons. Watch as they wave big and give each other a high-five. The sons have a dad, and here comes the dad now! Let's cheer as the dad enters the room! The dad thinks his sons are awesome and jumps to give them both a high-ten.

One day the younger son goes to his dad and begins moving his mouth up and down, and waving his arms around. He is telling his dad he wants his inheritance now and doesn't want to wait until his dad is old and about to die. This makes the dad sad. Watch as the dad makes a big sad face. Now watch as he reaches into his pockets and hands him a big wad of cash. This makes the son so happy. Watch as he jumps up and down, and waves goodbye to his dad and his brother. Now watch as the dad and the brother leave the room making sad faces.

The younger son is so excited; watch as he begins walking around the room looking for what to do with his money. Now entering the room is a salesperson; watch as she or he waves and runs over to the younger son. The salesperson has a great deal. Take a look at this awesome (whatever it is). Watch as the salesperson shows the son this cool item.

The son shrugs his shoulders, hands the salesperson some cash, and takes the whatever-it-is with him. The salesperson is so happy! Watch as she or he skips out of the room.

Next enters a chef with an awesome bag of snacks. These snacks are from a faraway country. Watch as the chef waves and hands the goodies to the younger son. The son shrugs his shoulders and pays for the food. The chef walks out with a big smile on his face.

This goes on and on, and the younger son keeps giving out money. Watch as the son hands money to the crowd until he has no more money left.

Now watch as the younger son makes a big sad face and rubs his tummy. He has no more food, no more money, and no more friends. What a lousy day. Finally, he ends up feeding pigs, and that is stinky. Watch as he plugs his nose.

One day the younger son decides to go home and see if his dad will let him work the farm. Watch as the son begins walking around.

When the dad sees his younger son, he runs to him and gives him a big high-five. I mean, a really big high-five. I mean, a really big high-five. He had missed his younger son and is so glad he is home. He has forgiven his son!

God is like the dad in this story, and we are like the son. When we mess up, God is always there to forgive us and give us a really big high-five!

Great job, everyone. Let's cheer for our actors!

Discussion Questions
1. How would you have felt if you asked for all of your inheritance?
2. How do you think the father felt when the younger son left?

Saul Follows Jesus

CHARACTERS: Saul, Followers of Jesus, Ananias, Light
SCRIPTURE: Acts 9
PROPS: flashlight

This is Saul. Saul is not being a very nice person. Watch as he makes a big mean face and then gives everyone a big thumbs-down.

Watch as some followers of Jesus enter the room and walk up to Saul and wave hello. Saul does not like these followers of Jesus at all. See him make a big mean face and point at the door. Saul is telling them to get out of here. Watch as the followers of Jesus leave the room and make big sad faces. Saul was pretty mean to them.

This is what Saul does all the time. He is mean to anyone who is following Jesus. Watch as Saul walks around the room, looking mean. Saul walks to different towns just to find people he can be mean to. Then one day, a bright light shines on Saul. See the light come into the room and shine in Saul's face.

The light is so bright, it makes Saul fall to his knees and close his eyes. The light is from the sky, and soon God speaks to Saul. God asks Saul why he was doing all the mean things.

Then God tells Saul that soon, someone will be by to help Saul. Watch as the bright light disappears. Now watch as Saul stands and tries to open his eyes. The bright light has left Saul blind; he can't see. Watch as Saul reaches out his hands and tries to find his way around.

Now entering the room is a follower of Jesus named Ananias. Ananias has been told by God to go help Saul. Watch as Ananias gives Saul a pat on the back, then pats his head.

Saul is blind for three days, then finally he can see again! Watch as Saul opens his eyes! Now watch as Ananias, the follower of Jesus, waves goodbye.

After being blind for three days, Saul has changed; watch as the followers of Jesus enter the room. This time, Saul gives everyone a high-five, a big thumbs-up, and a big smile.

Saul is changed after seeing the bright light and hearing God's voice on the road. He no longer tries to hurt those who follow Jesus. Instead, Saul becomes a follower and tells as many people as he can about Jesus. What an extreme change!

Great job, everyone. Let's cheer for our actors!

Discussion Questions
1. How do you think Saul felt when he could not see?
2. How do you think Saul felt when he heard God speak?

Washing Feet

CHARACTERS: Jesus, Disciples
SCRIPTURE: John 13:1-17
PROPS: chairs, box of cereal, juice boxes, bottle of water, towel

Sitting in the chairs today are the disciples of Jesus. Wave to us, Disciples! The disciples are having a great time at tonight's dinner party! Watch as they give everyone a big thumbs-up! Jesus is also at the dinner party. Jesus is the one waving to us right now.

Everyone is enjoying the cereal and juice boxes at dinner tonight. Watch as the disciples pass the cereal and the juice boxes around. Now watch as the disciples rub their bullies and say, "Yum!"

All of sudden, the disciples begin to smell something. Watch as they point to their noses, then give a big thumbs-down. Something really stinks! Watch as the disciples look up, then to the left, and then to the right to figure out what that horrible smell could be! They are not so sure what that smell is until they all look down at their feet!

Yikes! Their feet stink bad! Watch as the disciples hold their feet up in the air. Stinky!

You see, in Bible times, all the roads were dirt. People walked almost everywhere, and they wore sandals. Putting that all together makes for some really stinky feet.

It is proper at a fancy dinner party of cereal and juice boxes for the dinnertime servant to wash everyone's feet. But where is the dinnertime servant? Watch as the disciples look around and then shrug their shoulders.

Now watch as Jesus walks over to the bottle of water and the towel. What is Jesus doing? Watch as the disciples make big confused faces.

Now watch as Jesus grabs the bottle of water and towel, and begins washing the disciples' very stinky and very dirty feet. Watch as he moves down the line, wiping each foot carefully to be sure they are clean.

Wow! Jesus, the Son of God who came from heaven, is washing the disciples' feet!

Now watch as Jesus stands up and moves his mouth up and down, and waves his arms around. He is telling the disciples that they should follow his example and serve others.

Great job, everyone. Let's cheer for our actors!

Discussion Questions

1. How do you think the disciples felt when Jesus washed their feet?

2. How would you feel if Jesus washed your feet?

The Great Commission

CHARACTERS: Jesus, Disciples
SCRIPTURE: Matthew 28
PROPS: water bottles

Now entering the room is Jesus. Let's cheer for Jesus! Jesus also has a bunch of people who follow him and listen to everything he says. They are called disciples. Let's give a big cheer as the disciples enter the room.

Jesus spends a lot of time teaching the disciples what it means to believe in and follow God. Watch as Jesus moves his mouth up and down, and waves his arms around. That is good stuff, Jesus! Watch as the disciples give Jesus a big thumbs-up.

Jesus does a lot of walking, and pretty much wherever Jesus walks, the disciples follow. Watch as Jesus walks to one side of the room and the disciples follow him.

Then Jesus tells the disciples more cool stuff about God. Watch as he moves his mouth up and down, and waves his arms around. That is good stuff, Jesus! Watch as the disciples give Jesus a big thumbs-up.

Now watch as Jesus walks to the other side of the room and begins to move his mouth up and down, and wave his arms around. That is good stuff, Jesus! Watch as the disciples give Jesus a big thumbs-up.

OK, so this went on for three years. Little did the disciples know that Jesus was getting the disciples ready for a big mission.

One day Jesus takes the disciples to the top of a mountain. Watch as they climb the mountain. When they get to the top of the mountain, they are thirsty; watch as they take a drink from their water bottles.

Jesus has one final message for his followers. Watch as he waves his arms around, and moves his mouth up and down. Jesus is telling the disciples that he needs to go back to heaven, but now they must share the good news of God's love with everyone they can.

This is a big job. Watch as the disciples stretch their arms out. Now watch as the disciples make worried faces. Can they do this? Jesus tells them not to worry—the Holy Spirit will help them. Now watch as Jesus gives the disciples fist bumps and then waves goodbye. It's time for him to go back to heaven.

Now with Jesus gone, the disciples' mission begins. Watch as they face the crowd, point to the sky, move their mouths up and down, and wave their arms around.

The disciples began their mission and told everyone they could about Jesus. Now it is our turn to take this mission and share God's love with everyone we can.

Great job, everyone. Let's cheer for our actors!

Discussion Questions

1. How do you think the disciples felt when Jesus told them to share the good news?
2. How do you feel about sharing the good news?

Unmerciful Servant

CHARACTERS: King, Police Office, Servant 1, Servant 2
SCRIPTURE: Matthew 18:21-35
PROPS: crown, fake money, bag

Standing in front of you right now is the king. Let's all cheer for the king! The king is also a ninja; watch as the king shows us his best ninja move! The king is also very rich; watch as the king pulls some cash out of his bag. This is a lot of money, King!

Now entering the room is a police officer. Watch as the police officer claps his or her hands and in walks one of the king's servants. This servant looks really sad and really scared. Show us your best scared and sad face, Servant 1. Watch as the police officer waves his or her arms around, and moves his or her mouth up and down. The police officer is now pointing at the servant. The officer is telling the king that this servant owes the king one million dollars.

Wow! That is a big debt! And the servant does not have this much money. Watch as the servant begs for mercy. The servant gets down on her or his knees. The servant is asking the king to show a little kindness here. Watch as the king walks around the room, thinking. I wonder what the king is going to decide. The king has come to a decision.

Watch as the king walks over to the servant, shakes the servant's hand, and pats the servant on the back. Don't worry about the million dollars; it's no big deal. The servant is so happy! Watch as the servant jumps high in the air. I mean, really high in the air. I mean, really, really high in the air.

The king leaves the room, off to do some king stuff. Watch as the king waves goodbye. Watch as Servant 2 enters and walks around the back of the room, skipping. See Servant 1 tap the police officer on the head, and the officer brings Servant 2 to the middle of the room.

Watch as Servant 1 waves his or her arms around, and moves his or her mouth up and down. Servant 1 is telling Servant 2 that he or she owes him or her ten dollars, and Servant 2 better pay up right now.

OK. That is a small debt. But Servant 2 still does not have this much money. Watch as Servant 2 begs for mercy. Watch as Servant 2 gets down on his or her knees. The servant is asking Servant 1 to show a little kindness here.

Watch as Servant 1 walks around the room, thinking. I wonder what Servant 1 is going to decide. Servant 1 has decided—drumroll, please—to toss Servant 2 into prison. Watch as the police officer takes Servant 2 to jail.

Wait! What is going on here? What is Servant 1 doing? It didn't take the king very long to hear about what had happened. When the king hears this, he tosses Servant 1 in jail. The king is very sad about what Servant 1 has done.

In this story, God is the king, and we are the servant. God always shows us mercy, but we sometimes forget to show mercy and kindness to others.

Great job, everyone. Let's cheer for our actors!

Discussion Questions
1. How do you think the king felt when he forgave the debt of Servant 1?
2. How do you think Servant 2 felt when his debt was not forgiven?

CPSIA information can be obtained
at www.ICGtesting.com
Printed in the USA
LVOW03s1202081017

551525LV00001B/1/P